Surviving Your Adolescents

How to Manage
—and Let Go Of—
Your 13-to-18-Year-Olds

Surviving Your Adolescents

Thomas W. Phelan, Ph.D.

CHILD MANAGEMENT INC
Glen Ellyn, Illinois

Cover copy by Brett Jay Markel
Cover photography by Steve Orlick
Illustrations by Margaret Mayer
Child Management Logo by Steve Roe

Distributed by Login Publishers Consortium

Printed in the United States of America
10 9 8 7 6 5 4 3 2 1

For more information, contact:
Child Management, Inc.
800 Roosevelt Road
Glen Ellyn, Illinois 60137

Publisher's Cataloging-in-Publication
(Provided by Quality Books, Inc.)

Phelan, Thomas W., 1943-
    Surviving your adolescents / Thomas W. Phelan. -- 2nd ed.
    p. cm.
    ISBN: 1-889140-08-2

    1. Parent and teenager. 2. Parenting. 3. Child rearing.
I. Title.

HQ799.15.P44 1998   649'.125
                         QBI98-614

To the "kids,"

Tom and Julie

Contents

PART IV: EMOTIONAL BLACKMAIL

PART V: HOUSE RULES

PART VI: THE FUTURE

Introduction

L iving with a teenager is no picnic. There are times when you must bite your tongue as a child pushes towards independence. After all, the youngster is not supposed to live with you forever. There are also times, though, when you must intervene if you sense there is trouble.

Parents need to know when to be quiet and when to act. They also need to know what to do when something needs to be done. All these decisions come on top of the often perplexing job of getting along—and staying in touch with—the adolescent in the first place.

Surviving Your Adolescents is a practical guide for parents of adolescents in approximately the 13-to-18-year-old age bracket. It offers guidelines for handling the complex situations and dilemmas that teenagers often present. It is intended to be concrete and down-to-earth, offering specific suggestions—many of which can be applied immediately.

Many parents are interested in this program before their oldest child hits age 13. They want to prepare themselves for their children's adolescence. They want to learn what is normal behavior for a teenager and how they should respond.

Other parents are interested in *Surviving Your Adolescents* because

1

they already have teens and are aggravated by—or worried about—them. Mom and Dad may be concerned about "minor" problems such as arguing and sibling rivalry. On the other hand, they may be concerned about smoking, sexual activity or alcohol use.

Surviving Your Adolescents is, in a sense, a follow-up to *1-2-3 Magic: Effective Discipline for Children 2-12*. Many of the basic principles are similar, such as the No-Talking and No-Emotion Rules. To derive maximum benefit from *Surviving Your Adolescents,* parents may want to read *1-2-3 Magic* as well. In many ways, however, adolescents require different treatment than their younger counterparts, so you will find many new suggestions. Both books see parenting on a continuum, from taking charge to letting go. In general, the younger the children, the more parents need to take charge; the older the children, the more parents need to get used to letting go.

Surviving Your Adolescents also tries to recognize the fact that parents—especially parents of adolescents—do not possess infinite quantities of the following:

> Time
> Energy
> Skill
> Patience

Parents of teens have many problems to juggle. Many work full- or part-time. They also have to keep up the house, worry about their own aging parents, stay healthy and keep their spouses happy. And how about getting the car over for that new muffler?

With all these other concerns, parents don't need a parenting manual that is complicated, time-consuming and guilt inducing. They do need something that is straightforward and practical, offering specific "how to" advice.

Surviving Your Adolescents attempts to provide just that. We open by providing an orientation to adolescence in general. Teens and their parents are not from the same planet, and it is essential to know what to expect from normal teenagers. Some problems may be extremely aggravating but not very serious, while others may require professional attention.

Next we turn our attention to communication and safety. Most adolescents are going to take risks of many kinds during their teenage years, and Mom and Dad cannot accompany their kids every step of the way. While managing the troubled waters of romantic and sexual relationships, driving, drinking and other hazards, part of an adolescent's safety is dependent upon the extent to which she maintains positive and open communication with her parents. Parents must avoid—at all costs—what we call the "Four Cardinal Sins." Then, if they have any time and energy left, there are several specific suggestions for maintaining or improving a relationship with a teenage son or daughter. Some of these suggestions can be acted on immediately, but none of them is easy.

We then discuss what parents should do when they are concerned or aggravated by their teenage son or daughter's behavior. First, the middle-aged parent needs to have a feel for his own state of mind and his own well-being if he is to interact positively with his kids and avoid the emotional dumping that can sometimes lead to a virtual state of war. Parents can consider four possible roles when they are concerned about something. These roles vary from doing nothing (Observer) to taking charge (Director), and it is important that a parent give careful thought to matching the chosen role to the problem. Teenagers do not take kindly to unnecessary interference!

We also discuss how a parent should respond if he finds his teen is engaging in some of the more serious risk-taking behaviors, such as careless driving, drinking and/or drug use and sexual activity.

When Mom and Dad have to do something assertive in their child's interest, few teens will thank their parents. So we next look at the Six Kinds of Testing and Manipulation—the teens' efforts to confuse their parents, muddle the real issues, and get their way. Clear recommendations for handling testing are provided.

House Rules suggests some concrete ideas for managing some of the more common—but less risky—problems that adolescents present to their parents. This section also gives some specific examples of how to apply the principles and methods discussed earlier in the book. The problems include:

Arguing	Music
Bedtime	Meals and eating habits
Bumming around town	Messy rooms
Car: care, use, gas	Money, allowance, loans
Chores	Negative attitude
Church	Parties: home and away
Clothes, hair, earrings	Phone
College plans	Sibling rivalry
Depression	Smoking cigarettes
Family outings	Swearing
Friends and dating	School (behavioral trouble)
Grades	Using your things
Grammar	Vacations
Homework	Work
Hours	

Finally, *Surviving Your Adolescents* takes a look at the future. Did you ever stop to think that an 18-year-old is just 12 years away from being 30? That length of time may sound like an eternity right now, but for most of us, those years speed by all too quickly.

This book is not intended to be a replacement for counseling or psychotherapy. We will clearly define problems for which a professional evaluation is necessary. In fact, many people have found that the ideas in *Surviving Your Adolescents* are helpful when integrated into psychological treatment, especially since these ideas do not require the parent to be a genius, saint or professional psychotherapist in order to apply them.

As with *1-2-3 Magic*, the methods presented here are also based upon the actual experiences of parents, as well as the author's own parenting and clinical work. A very large number of these parents had to deal with Attention Deficit Disorder children, one of the hardest groups there is to manage. The techniques described here, therefore, are quite practical and down-to-earth. ADD kids don't give you much room to monkey around, and there is a lot of truth to the statement, "If you can handle an ADD child, you can handle anybody!"

Parent of adolescent. There is no magical cure for this difficult condition. It is, however, short-lived. We hope that *Surviving Your Adolescents* will help you—and your teenagers—live through this time as pleasantly and productively as possible.

Part I

A Different Planet

1

Adolescence in America

The vast majority of adults vividly remember their own teenage years. The first thing they usually recall is the social scene they felt they were a part of. Then again, they may recall the social scene from which they felt excluded. Peer relationships were extremely important. Who was cool? Who was cute? Who was a geek or a nerd?

There may be no other time in life when a person's social sensitivity is as intense as it is during adolescence. Negotiating and maintaining same-sex friendships was critical. You wanted to have some friends to hang out with during and after school. It was fun to get together with people your own age, and it also helped to have others with whom you could talk to try to make sense out of these bewildering years. And—on pain of psychological death—you absolutely had to have someone to sit with at lunchtime in the cafeteria.

Plunked right on top of the difficult task of making and keeping friends was the exciting and totally confusing problem of the opposite sex. While you had been asleep, it seemed, romantic appeal suddenly emerged as an all-too-important dimension of your self-esteem. What do I look like? What kind of personality do I have? Who's going to pay attention to me? Some people seemed to be getting along OK, but some obviously were not. This whole new scene was kind of scary, but you were always aware that on the outside you must never appear uncertain or vulnerable. You had to act like the whole thing was just a piece of cake.

Complicating the picture was the internal agenda that said you had to prove something. Suddenly, it seemed, you were supposed to be somebody and you were supposed to make something of yourself. But what exactly was it you were supposed to prove, or what were you supposed to be? Academic achievement was OK if you were up to it, but good grades weren't always considered cool. Having a job helped, gave you your own funds, and increased your sense of independence. For those who could swing the deal, having your own car was also pretty neat— especially if there was a girlfriend to go in it.

During the junior and senior years, issues of college and career became more and more pressing. What am I going to do with the rest of my life? Who am I going to do it with?

Meanwhile, parents and family were becoming such a drag. You definitely did not want to be seen in public with your parents. Older people were such nerds sometimes, and their ideas were positively ancient. Mom and Dad couldn't seem to shake the notion that you were still only about eight years old and incapable of managing your own affairs. Parents talked about "responsibility" all the time, but they didn't ever really give you any—other than cleaning your room or taking out the garbage. Siblings, as well, were often a total pain, and they *never* gave you any respect.

Everyone remembers his or her adolescence. Every day it felt as though a lot was at stake, and there were many times when you wished you could get this part of your life over with as quickly as possible—and leap into adulthood.

Prolonged Dependence

Not so fast. Adding insult to injury for most adolescents is the fact that their teenage years last so long. Adolescence for many "youngsters" is not simply the ages 13 to 18; it really encompasses the years from age 11 (for many the onset of puberty) to age 22 (the completion of college). During these years the young man or woman is still dependent upon parents and others for food, shelter, clothing and warmth, as well as for direction and supervision. This situation may persist even though the young person may be biologically and mentally capable of managing a lot more himself.

Of all the animals on earth, the human spends the largest portion of its total life span (approximately one third) with its parents before achieving final independence. Bugs, fish, birds and even monkeys live with their parents for only a relative fraction of the time that human offspring do. And of all the countries on earth, the more modern, industrialized nations—such as the United States—keep their kids under foot for the longest period of time. This longer dependence is largely due to the extended time required to educate children for the more compli- cated, skilled jobs and careers that are characteristic of industrial coun- tries. For most there is first a high school diploma, then an associate's degree or bachelor's degree. And how about an MBA or a Ph.D.?

Long ago, Margaret Mead pointed out that in simpler societies the transition from childhood to adulthood was usually much shorter. Anthro- pologists also have found that in a few cultures, "adolescence" doesn't exist at all. One day you're a kid, and then wham!, after a brief ceremony or "rite of passage," you're an adult—ready or not—with all the privileges and responsibilities of other adults in your community.

But in the United States, as well as other modern nations, privilege and responsibility are dished out piecemeal to the new adult/child between the approximate ages of 13 and 21. Now you can manage your own money and choose your own clothes. Now you can drive. Now you can date, go to work or leave school. Now you can legally vote or drink or stay out past midnight. What about sex? You are supposed to delay sexual gratification for a long, long time.

Insult

Most teens, however, feel they're ready for adult responsibilities and privileges long before parents and society are willing to let the adolescents tackle them. For some kids these youthful perceptions may be correct, while for others these views may be way off-base. Nevertheless, the inevitable result of the prolonged dependence of adolescence in our culture is a that—from time to time—teens are bound to feel a certain amount of resentment toward their elders. They will feel insulted because they are still supervised, restricted and not allowed to do the things they feel they are capable of doing. Whether their perception is correct or incorrect, some irritation is inevitable.

Teens will also feel an urge to rebel, do things differently and criticize the ways of their parents and other adults. This oppositional stance is one way for them to both maintain their self-respect—while still in a semi-dependent state—and to distance themselves from their often-unwanted caretakers. After all, teens are supposed to be becoming more and more independent. Often these rebellious urges will involve incredibly annoying but harmless activities. At other times, however, these impulses will result in truly dangerous, risk-taking behavior. Part of a parent's job is to know the difference.

While resentment and rebelliousness are usually a necessary part of adolescence, they are not often horribly destructive, nor are they usually constant. Much of the time adolescents can tolerate their dependent, "in-between" status reasonably well. They are able—most of the time, anyway—to enjoy themselves, get along with their parents (though not necessarily with their siblings!), and stay out of trouble.

2

What Is Normal?

One of the toughest parts of being the parent of a teenager is trying to figure out which aspects of your kids' behavior are trouble and which are normal. Some days it seems that most of what teens do is strange, aggravating and worlds apart from the way they used to act. What ever happened to that easygoing nine-year-old whom I used to enjoy so much?

In this chapter we'll describe the characteristics you can reasonably expect to see in your normal, average teenager. Anticipating these can help you in several ways. First of all, it tells you that these new traits are not necessarily dangerous. Second, knowing what's normal can allow you to not take these qualities personally—as if they were your fault, or as if they represented some kind of personal rejection. Finally, memorizing this list will get you to work on one of the primary jobs of the parent of an adolescent: *toleration of nonessential differences.*

Change

Adolescence is a time of massive, multiple changes. Some of these changes take years, while others seem to occur almost overnight. Some changes are exciting, while others may be bewildering or even upsetting for teens and parents alike.

Physically the body of an adolescent will change more than it will at any other time of life except infancy. From the beginning to the end of puberty, adolescents on the average add ten inches in height and 40 pounds in weight. The growth spurt for girls begins around age 11, on the average, and is completed by age 16. Girls' hips broaden relative to their shoulders and waist, and they tend to add more fat on their arms, legs and torso. The growth spurt for boys starts around age 13 and continues until about age 171/2. Boys' shoulders broaden relative to their waists, and they develop larger skeletal muscles while decreasing arm and leg fat.

During puberty the sex hormones start to do their thing. Perspiration, oiliness of the skin and hair, and body odor all increase. Sex hormones also see to it that primary and secondary sexual characteristics develop. Teens do not always greet these physical events with enthusiasm. Girls react to the arrival of their first period with surprise and mixed emotions which depend, in part, upon how much support they receive from family members and how much prior information they have. Boys usually have more advance information before they experience their first ejaculation, but in general they receive less support for the physical changes of puberty than do girls.

While the physical changes mentioned above take a few years, it may seem to parents that some of the other changes we'll describe in this chapter occur overnight. One day, without warning, the child's bedroom door shuts and stays shut. During one summer month the youngster seems to have become glued to a new set of friends, and suddenly he couldn't care less about family affairs.

Sometimes adolescent change goes back and forth. One day the kid is friendly, warm and fun. The next day he is moody and distant for no identifiable reason. You have a hard time making sense out of his frequent bouts of ambivalence. To paraphrase the title of one recent book about teenagers: "Get out of my life, but first drive me to the mall!"

Whatever the case, change is a large part of the teen years, and Mom and Dad's understanding and tolerance of the non-dangerous alterations in their offsprings' appearance, thinking and behavior is an important part of the tricky new art of parenting.

Weirdness

Make no bones about it: teenagers are weird! They love weirdness, shock value, strange sounds, colors and clothes. Being different—from adults, not from each other—becomes an important goal in their daily activities. Forging an identity does not mean slavish imitation of your own mother or father.

While in a grocery check-out line one day, I was struck by the appearance of the young girl who was ringing up the orders. Though she had a very pleasant personality, her hair was amazingly unconventional. Half of her head was sporting a blue crew cut, while the other half had spiked, orange hair. While gazing at this remarkable display I found myself trying to decide if she had been pretty before she had done this to herself.

It may be true that all generations think the music of next generation is weird. My parents thought Elvis Presley was extremely odd and almost immoral, while my friends and I loved his music. Now I myself don't like "rap" and cannot understand how anyone would ever want to listen to it in the first place.

Among teens, army jackets have to some extent been replaced by clothes that are pretty much falling off their owners' bodies. Boys' haircuts appear to have been done by placing a bowl over the head and simply shaving around the edge. Pierced ears—by themselves—are now old-fashioned. The new trend is to pierce—apparently as many times as you can—anything made of flesh that protrudes. Noses, tongues, eyebrows, navels. And a body part doesn't have to stick out far to qualify as a target.

Distance

Parents will find that their teens are becoming more and more distant from them, both physically and emotionally. The child doesn't want to eat dinner with the family as often as before. She is less interested in going out with you as well, whether it's for dinner, to a movie or for family get-togethers.

Privacy becomes more important to the adolescent. Her door is now shut more of the time, and you're left wondering what's going on in there now that wasn't happening before. It's certainly not all homework. The meanderings of younger brothers or sisters into your teenage daughter's bedroom may be met with bursts of temper and demands to be left alone.

Communication also isn't the same. Where you used to sit around and shoot the breeze after dinner, now the kid is gone without having said hardly anything. It doesn't seem she tells you as much as before about things that bother—or excite—her, though she appears to be able to talk on the phone for hours with friends. Innocent questions such as "How was your day?" are often met with an attitude of irritation or suspicion, as if you were unjustly prying into her affairs.

Your daughter is showing more and more independence. For one thing, she is simply not home as much as before. It's nice she has a job, but between that and her friends, you hardly ever see her. Your suggestion that the two of you go out shopping for clothes is met with an icy stare. She'd rather do that on her own.

Peers

Your child's social focus has shifted dramatically away from home and toward friends. During his spare time he wants to go out with his buddies. He seems to have little time for family, or for you, or for doing what he's supposed to around the house. Essential tasks like cutting the grass don't get done, but there seems to be plenty of time for frivolous encounters with friends. Half of these kids you haven't even met, and some of those you have met you're not at all sure you like.

When a relationship with the opposite sex develops, it is positively obsessive. Long and extremely private conversations on the phone are followed by starry-eyed wonder or unexplained moodiness. The question "Is there something wrong?" inspires a snarl and a not-too-gentle hint that you should mind your own business. When—God forbid—a romantic relationship ends after months of breakups and tearful reunions, you find yourself unable to sleep at night, worrying about depression and suicidal potential.

Inexperience

The teenage years are a time of great excitement as well as great turmoil. Part of the excitement comes from what the teen sees as the unlimited possibilities ahead. The mind of the adolescent, therefore, is occupied more with dreams than experience. The dreams are endless and, in a sense, always instantly available. On the other hand, the dreams are not realities yet, yielding an often painful sense of inferiority and lack of identity. The career that may come later does not exist now and may not even be chosen; the family (spouse and kids) one may create later is not here now.

In contrast to the parent, the adolescent mental state may look something like this:

The result is that adolescents spend a lot of time daydreaming. Their whole life is before them, and they like to imagine what it will be like. The psychological pain that may result from the current lack of fulfillment can be partially managed by such fantasies. Since teens have not had a lot of experience yet in testing these dreams against reality, many of their notions may seem crazy to their parents.

The inexperience of adolescence does not mean that teens have no opinions. On the contrary, they can be quite opinionated as well as idealistic. Someone once said, "If you want to get something done, give it to a teenager while they still know everything." Teens have quite a few ideas about how the world—as well as their family, school and country— should be run. They may come across as budding trial attorneys when they evaluate the activities of their elders. That's why one of the top complaints from parents about their teenage sons and daughters is that the kids argue too much.

Self-Consciousness

Younger adolescents become extremely focused on their own thoughts, feelings and activities. In fact, some writers have pointed out that it's almost as if the child feels she is constantly on stage in front of some imaginary audience. She may feel that her own experiences are so intense and unique that no one else—least of all her parents—could possibly understand what she is going through. In feeling misunderstood teens forget that their parents were adolescents once too. In a sense, though, the kids have a point, because many parents react impulsively to their adolescent offspring and don't take the time to recall what it was like when they were that age. Parents may complain that "she's too wrapped up in her own little world" without remembering what that "little world" was like for them a long time ago.

The other side of self-consciousness, of course, is egocentricity: the whole world is watching and everything revolves around me. This orientation toward life is definitely a mixed blessing. The adolescent may feel that her successes are marvelous and amazing—testimonials to her incredible potential. On the other hand, failure and being criticized in front of others can be excruciating. "That's just great. Now everyone will think I'm a total dork!"

Risk-Taking

Adolescents take risks. They are experimenters. We worry about their driving, drug use, smoking, drinking and sexual activity. Teens can be dangerously creative. One study of adolescent mortality, for example, reported a number of teenage deaths due to skateboarding under the influence of alcohol.

Some adolescent risk-taking, of course, is due to a natural, healthy curiosity about life. There are so many fascinating new experiences to be discovered! Teenage experimentation also results from the urge to do things differently from one's parents. "Mom and Dad are such a drag sometimes; don't they ever have any fun? I'm going to do things my way and enjoy life."

Some risk-taking also results from the egocentric adolescent view that one has unique awareness and special abilities that will not allow injury. Even though teens are at a point where they can intellectually appreciate the possible consequences of certain behavior, they don't always "put two and two together" when it comes down to their own actions. Sadly, every year thousands of teen pregnancies and auto fatalities are caused, in part, by this unfounded sense of invulnerability.

Risk-taking behavior in adolescents is both normal and frightening. One study, for example, found evidence to support the idea that periodic acting-out behavior during the teenage years—as long as a child doesn't "O.D." on it—may actually reflect a normal, healthy adolescent personality. This research looked at three groups of teens: those who used marijuana heavily during high school, those who only experimented with it, and those who never tried it. Using psychological tests and interview data, these groups were later evaluated, as young adults, with regard to their overall emotional health.

What was found was that the kids who experimented with marijuana as adolescents were—when evaluated later—better emotionally adjusted than those who had never tried anything. Not surprisingly, the experimenters were also better emotionally adjusted than the group who had used marijuana regularly (this last group was found to be the most disturbed). The point is not, of course, an endorsement for drug use. What the study suggests is that some experimentation is normal—it's going to happen (we'll provide some specific statistics later).

Risk-taking, by itself, then, is not necessarily a sign of emotional disturbance. A parent's job is to realize that experimentation is normal while at the same time trying to discourage its dangerous forms. Not an easy task at all! In Chapter 4 we'll provide some specific data regarding teenage experimentation and risk-taking.

Variation Among Teens

Not all teenagers, of course, will exactly fit the description of "normal" adolescents that we have just proposed. Along the lines of the study we just mentioned, you might think of teens as very roughly falling into three categories: Straight Arrows, Experimenters and Seriously Disturbed. The middle group, the Experimenters, is what we just tried to describe as the "normal" teenager.

What you see in the Straight Arrows are fewer of the characteristics that tend to grate on parents' nerves. While these kids may feel just as self-conscious inside and may be just as inexperienced as the other groups, the Straight Arrows show no sudden changes, less slow change, and less weirdness. They are less independent, more inclined to stay involved with the family, and less critical of their parents. Arguing and risk-taking in this group are minimal.

While the Straight Arrows are less aggravating, they may not be as emotionally well-adjusted as the Experimenters. The normal teenager aggravates his parents on a fairly regular basis. The irony here is that if you have a teenage child who doesn't worry or aggravate you at all, perhaps you should be worried! Take this with a grain of salt, of course, because many kids who are Straight Arrows on the outside are doing just fine. Others, however, may be far too shy, withdrawn or depressed.

The Seriously Disturbed group, on the other hand, aggravates and worries their parents far too often. They are extremely weird, rebellious and argumentative. With regard to driving, drugs and sex, these kids take serious risks on a regular basis, but their parents don't know the half of it. These teens are inexperienced and actually naive, but they come across as egocentric, totally independent and cocky. They are very involved with friends whom their parents have either never met or whom they don't like.

A parent's job can be complicated by what "types" of adolescents they get and in what order they get them. Imagine your first teen was of the Disturbed variety. You got baptized early. If your next child turns out to be a normal Experimenter, she will feel to you like a Straight Arrow. What a relief! And if your first adolescent was Seriously Disturbed and your next one turned out to be a Straight Arrow, she must have felt like a gift from heaven.

On the other hand, what if your first was a Straight Arrow? You got spoiled and perhaps developed some unrealistic expectations about what average teens are like. If your next child turned out to be an Experimenter, you may have seen him as Seriously Disturbed and in need of psychological treatment. And what about a Disturbed teen who follows a Straight Arrow? This sequence is tailor-made to drive parents crazy.

3

Is It Serious?

It's very difficult to think about a teen objectively. Then again, it's not so easy being objective about yourself, either. Many people in our culture suffer from self-esteem problems because they don't know how to evaluate themselves properly. In a moment we're going to ask you to evaluate your teenager, but first we need to provide a short course in straight thinking. Otherwise you may get off on the wrong foot.

Why should you take a moment to get a better perspective on your teenager? For one thing, it's all too easy to focus on one or two aggravating problems so much that you lose your perspective on your child. Evaluating "your" adolescent objectively may help you relax. On the other hand, perhaps you're missing or ignoring some serious trouble.

Objectivity: The "Nine-and-One" Rule

If you do ten things in the course of a day, nine of them right and one of them wrong, which do you think about at the end of the day? The one you goofed up! That seems reasonable enough, doesn't it? But some people take this line of thinking further and come to the conclusion that because of their recent performance they must be idiots or jerks.

This is not reasonable, but it's a very common way of thinking. What the person does here is base his opinion of himself on only a small portion of his overall behavior. Some people refer to this as "overgeneralization," otherwise known as making a mountain out of a molehill. But the fact of the matter is that most of us are much more impressed by the things that we do wrong than by the things that we do right. There is probably some biological base to this which may have its foundations in the evolutionary development of human beings. Wouldn't it be nice to have a species of animal that was continually problem-focused and always on the lookout for trouble, whose members never just sat around wasting time feeling good about what they had accomplished?

Maybe. That species would certainly be very durable and adaptable. But you might not want to be a member of it! You would always be torturing yourself about everything you were not doing right, while you continually took for granted everything you did well. Since you could never be perfect, you would be set up for a life of mental self-abuse.

This self-torture is exactly what many—or perhaps most—human beings engage in. If they do nine of ten things correctly, they abuse themselves about the one they did wrong. They conclude that they are idiots.

Let's turn the situation around, but use the same logic. Imagine a day in which you do ten different things, nine of them wrong and only one right, and that evening you come to the conclusion that you are Super-woman or Superman. Doesn't that seem dumb? Most people, oddly enough, will agree that this example doesn't make sense, but they have a much harder time seeing the lack of logic involved in concluding that they are incompetent when only a small portion of their actions are faulty.

The conclusion? Your self-esteem should be based upon a realistic and fair perception of yourself. If, in fact, you are doing most of what you should reasonably well, if most of what you are doing is constructive (including having fun!) and if in general you are taking care of business and getting along with most people most of the time, you probably qualify as a basically decent and competent person. Your self-esteem—if you remain matter-of-fact—should not crumble if one day your performance is not perfect.

Part of the reason for going into this issue here is this: if you evaluate yourself unfairly using unrealistic rules, you will also tend to evaluate other family members unfairly. If you apply the standards of perfectionism and overgeneralization to your teens, you will be much more impressed, angered, hurt, etc., by their bad behavior and tend to take for granted their good behavior—which for most kids is 90 percent of what they do. When we ask you in just a moment to evaluate your son or daughter, try to keep this in mind.

What Child Is This?

Although it is admittedly difficult to generalize about a human being, we actually do it all the time. Comments like "She's a great kid," "I can't stand that moron," or "You'd better get your act together" all reflect our tendency to generalize about our children.

So if you're going to generalize (not overgeneralize) about your son or daughter, let's try to do it as fairly and objectively as possible. Keeping in mind the "Nine-and-One" Rule and taking everything into account, how is your adolescent doing with his or her life right now? Do you think of your child as competent, sort of average, or as a problem child?

For example, the competent child (not necessarily a Straight Arrow) gets along fairly well with her family and presents few discipline problems. She can maintain close friends as well as acquaintances, she enjoys school and is working just about up to her capability. At work she is responsible and thought of positively by her supervisor and coworkers. She feels reasonably OK about herself (keep in mind that the self-esteem of an adolescent should be a little bit shaky).

The teen you might consider average gets along OK in the family for the most part, but he can present significant problems and turmoil at times. He has some friends, though you may not always care for them. The child feels so-so about school and academically operates at, or a little below, his potential. If he has a job, he works off and on, is fairly reliable, and has occasional minor problems with supervisors. This teen has times when he feels he's not so hot (whether or not this is said out loud), but does not seem to be overly self-critical most of the time.

The youngster you might think of as a problem child is distant, hostile, and often argumentative at home. You may love him but you have difficulty liking him. He is a loner or hangs out with kids you dislike intensely and who you feel are bad influences on him. He hates school and works well below his overall intellectual ability. He either doesn't work or gets fired or quits a lot, and has trouble with supervision. Though defensive and never prone to taking negative feedback graciously, you always imagine that he has a poor self image.

Remember that this evaluation process is certainly not perfect or exact. In reality, the result will probably be some combination of subjectivity and objectivity. But it is very important to take a long, hard, realistic look at your offspring rather than thinking impulsively about them and then shooting from the hip when attempting to solve problems. Is your child really as bad as you have been thinking, or were you being a little perfectionistic? What are this child's strengths? On the other hand, do problems exist in just one area of his life, or are there many areas of concern? Are there problems that are really worse than you want to admit?

Your Teens Have Their MBAs!

Take just a minute to make sure you have your perspective on something else: how serious are the different types of problems your adolescents come up with? If you stop to think about it, not all problems are created equal.

Many things that adolescents do—or don't do—fall into the "MBA" category. That means they are Minor But Aggravating. It's very important for parents to keep in mind that their level of aggravation about a problem is not always a measure of the seriousness of that problem. Just because you get ferociously angry about something, in other words, doesn't mean it is a sign of a major character flaw, mental illness or sociopathic tendencies in your offspring. It may be just one irritating part of normal adolescence.

What kinds of problems fall into the MBA category? One of the best examples is the use of the phone. Do you know that long, pointless and apparently stupid conversations between teenagers over the phone are normal and healthy? Endless dialogues are what kids are supposed to be doing at this age!

The phone rings and your 16-year-old daughter dives for it. The following conversation ensues:

"Hello."
"Hi. What are you doing?"
"Nothing. What are you doing?"
"Nothing."
"Cool."

Two hours later not much more of significance is being discussed, but everything's still cool. You, however, are not cool. You begin fuming, thinking about your phone bill, and about how your daughter could better spend her time doing extra-credit work for biology.

Relax. Conversations like this are good for kids. They are making contact with each other. They are learning how to handle relationships. These connections are good for their self-esteem. Would you rather they weren't talking to anyone?

If you're concerned about the phone bill, make a deal that the kids pay for any charges over a certain amount per month. Otherwise, leave them alone or don't listen.

Another MBA-type "problem" has to do with dress and appearance. This issue involves clothing, hair, earrings and other attachments to the body. It's not reasonable to expect your teens to want to dress like you. Remember, part of their thinking is that they often want to look as different from you as possible.

One solution to the appearance problem: the kids can wear anything that the school will let them in the door with. Of course, schools' criteria are not too strict these days, but this policy does offer some control.

Another MBA? That messy room. What a pit! Your stomach writhes in agony every time you look at it. Do you know that there are no studies that prove that teens with messy rooms grow up to be homeless persons or schizophrenics, or have a higher divorce rate than the rest of the population?

What's the solution? It may be to close the door and don't look. Or leave the door open and close your eyes as you go past. A sloppy bedroom is aggravating, but it isn't really a major problem or a sure indicator of deep psychological trouble. Also, be realistic. If all the nagging and arguing and lecturing you've done over the years hasn't convinced your 17-year-old son to clean his room regularly, he isn't going to start now no matter what you do. We respectfully suggest that you have lost the battle. It's not the end of the world, and you don't want arguing about a messy room to be the end of your relationship.

If you already have your own rules about the MBAs we just discussed, and your rules are working just fine, pay no attention to the advice here. What does "working just fine" mean? Two things. First, the rules are not unreasonably restrictive. Second, the rules do not result in a lot of nagging, arguing or lecturing.

Other MBAs

Here are some other probable Minor-But-Aggravating issues that you might consider staying away from:

Musical preferences	Eating habits
Grammar	Use of allowance
Not going on family outings	Using your things
Intermittent negative attitude	Forgetfulness with chores

Certainly these problems can all be aggravating—in fact, very aggravating—but they should not necessarily be taken as indications that your child is emotionally disturbed. Remember this cardinal rule for parents of adolescents—especially as the kids get older: never open your mouth unless you have a very good reason.

On the list of other *possible* MBAs are things like arguing, bedtime, swearing and bumming around town. These items may or may not be serious, depending on your situation. They are usually less serious the more competent your teenager is, the better your relationship with the child is, and the better you are doing yourself.

By the way, can you guess which two problems bug parents the most? Not drugs and drinking, not even smoking. In our surveys the "winners" are consistently arguing and sibling rivalry. This fact does not, of course, mean they are the most serious—simply the most frequently infuriating.

What Are Not MBAs?

Adolescence is difficult enough for kids and their parents, but sometimes certain psychological problems—which are definitely not MBAs—are added to the picture. These can cause intense suffering for adolescents as well as their parents. Parents should not try to manage these difficulties on their own; professional evaluation and counseling are usually essential (see Chapter 13 for more information). These more serious, non-MBA problems include the following:

Anxiety Disorders: some children are biologically predisposed to have excessive fears. These anxieties can relate to social situations, separation, obsessive thoughts and life in general.

Depression: true clinical depression involves a consistently gloomy view of life and, in adolescents, persistent irritability. It lowers self-esteem, takes the joy out of things, and is often accompanied by appetite and sleeping disturbances, social withdrawal and underachievement.

Attention Deficit Disorder: definitely the most common childhood and adolescent problem. The poor concentration skills and frequent intense temperaments of these children can affect all areas of their lives—at school, at home, and with peers.

Conduct Disorder: perhaps a euphemism for what used to be called "juvenile delinquency." CD kids are defiant, abuse the rights of others, and prematurely act out in areas such as sex, drugs, stealing and fighting. These children blame everyone else for their problems.

Eating Disorders: anorexic girls refuse to maintain a normal body weight and have very distorted images of their own bodies, seeing fat where none exists. Bulimics can maintain a normal weight but often engage in binge-purge routines that jeopardize their physical health and trigger intense shame.

Alcohol and Drug Abuse: it is common for teens to experiment with alcohol and marijuana. Some, however, overuse these substances or use them in combination on a regular basis. A major problem exists when the drug use becomes a central life activity for the adolescent, especially when this use interferes with school, social, work and family life.

Divorce-Related Problems: kids are resilient, but recent evidence suggests that parents' divorce can be especially traumatic for some children. When remarriages are involved, adolescents are harder to merge into the "blended family," sometimes causing extreme stress on second marriages.

Sexual Abuse: estimates of the percentage of girls who have been sexually abused vary widely, but there is no doubt the number is high. The effects on a child can range from precocious sexual activity to chronic guilt, poor interpersonal relationships and low self-esteem.

Worrisome and irritating adolescent behaviors are not all the same. Take a moment to reflect. Perhaps you've been having fits about some relatively minor things. On the other hand, perhaps you've been ignoring a problem with which you and your child need professional assistance.

Part II

Communication
and
Safety

4

Risky Business

A dolescents take chances that range from the trivial to the sublime. They may be curious to see what happens if they cut a class or stay up all night. They may try out some new clothes, a new hair style, or even a different kind of personality for a while. But by far the most dangerous risk-taking teens engage in involves the "Big Three": driving, drug and alcohol use, and sex. Armed with their new sense of invulnerability and the idea that "it can't happen to me, " adolescents get injured and killed—or injure and kill others—with alarming frequency.

On the Road

Each year motor vehicle accidents by themselves account for almost 40 percent of adolescent deaths. We sometimes forget this gruesome statistic, but insurance companies do not. They charge their highest rates for the riskiest group of drivers—adolescent males—and their rates go even higher if the boy in question is not a particularly good student.

Teenage deaths due to automobile accidents involve more than just teenage drivers. They also include the passengers of adolescent-driven cars and motorcycles, as well as the pedestrians and the bicyclists—old as well as young—whom these kids kill or cripple.

Teens are thrilled by the excitement, freedom and independence involved in being able to take the car out by themselves without Mom or Dad. Unfortunately, at the time they acquire this privilege these children have had precious little driving experience. Yet lack of driving experience may not be so much of a factor in teen traffic fatalities as risky driving habits. Teens are famous for not using seatbelts, for speeding and for tailgating.

Adolescents are also known for drinking and driving. When a motor vehicle accident involves a fatality and a teenage driver, that driver has a blood alcohol level of 0.1 percent or above 50 percent of the time. Use of alcohol as well as other drugs also plays an all-too-frequent role when teens die in accidents involving recreational vehicles. In one study, one-fifth of high school seniors—the vast majority male—said they had either driven after drinking or ridden with a drinking driver three or more times during the last year.

Drugs and Alcohol

Teenagers are fascinated with alcohol. What is this stuff that our parents use so regularly and that can change behavior so dramatically? What does it feel like to be high or smashed? Do you have more fun or do you just get sick? Can alcohol give you more self-confidence?

This curiosity, combined with the encouragement of peers and factors such as low socioeconomic status, poor school performance, parental drug use and lack of close friends, has resulted in extremely high adolescent use of alcohol and other drugs in the United States—higher than in any other industrialized country. By the time they are 14 years old, 50 percent of our kids have tried drinking. By the time they are seniors in high school, four percent of students are daily drinkers. In one suburban high school survey, 37 percent of seniors said they had used alcohol three or more times in the last month, or had gotten drunk one or more times in the last two weeks. Fifteen percent of eighth graders said the same about themselves.

Smoking and the effects of nicotine also fascinate kids. By the time they hit age 14, 42 percent of our youngsters have tried smoking cigarettes, and by the time they are seniors, 15 percent are regular cigarette smokers.

Adolescent use of illegal drugs is also extremely high in the U.S. as compared to other countries. These drugs include marijuana, amphetamines, cocaine, crack, PCP, heroin and others. By age 14, 23 percent of our kids have tried at least one illegal drug—usually marijuana. By the time they leave high school, well over half have experimented with illegal substances. In the suburban study mentioned earlier, 38 percent of seniors said they had used illegal drugs three or more times in the last twelve months. The list of drugs in this study included cocaine, LSD, PCP, heroin and amphetamines.

Sex

While growing up in the United States, a typical youngster will see on prime-time TV an average of three episodes per hour that involve spontaneous, romantic and unprotected sex. Advertisers exploit sex constantly on television, in magazines and in newspapers. Our society is enthralled with sex, but at the same time—believe it or not—the United States is much more conservative about sex than many other countries. Parents in this country rarely talk about sex to, or in front of, their children, and they rarely give the kids much information about sex. Consequently, children turn to sources such as movies, magazines and friends, where the quality of the information they receive is unpredictable.

What are the consequences of being a teenager, with your hormones going full blast and living in a sexually overstimulated society that refuses to discuss sex openly? Adolescents get hurt in two ways: unwanted pregnancy and sexually transmitted diseases.

The United States has the highest adolescent pregnancy rate of any industrialized nation—unfortunately by a long ways. Our rate is three times that of England, Canada or France. Each year over one million teens become pregnant—the vast majority of them unmarried. Forty percent of these girls decide on abortion as the solution, and another 13 percent of the pregnancies result in miscariage. Surprisingly, very few teens choose to give up their babies for adoption, with the result that every year over

300,000 unmarried teenage girls become parents under the most difficult of circumstances and their babies enter the world at serious risk.

The other sex-related problem that causes consistent injury to teens is sexually transmitted disease. Adolescents in this country have the highest rate of STD of any age group. This statistic does not mean that all teens here are sexually promiscuous, though some certainly are. The rate of sexual activity in the United States is similar to that of other industrialized nations: by the time they are eighteen years old, according to one study, 64 percent of boys and 44 percent of girls will have been sexually active—but usually with only one partner at a time.

Kids get into trouble with sexually transmitted diseases for other reasons. For one thing, convenient, non-embarrassing and low-cost access to birth control devices is rare. Providing condoms or birth control pills to teens is also a very controversial issue. But even when protection is available, teens don't always use it. As we have mentioned before, though they are sometimes capable of visualizing the consequences of their actions, when it comes right down to it teens don't always "put two and two together."

The most serious of the sexually transmitted diseases is AIDS, which is on the rise as a major cause of death among young adults. Because this disease takes a few years to develop, however, adolescents who contract it don't usually die of AIDS during their teenage years. Most new cases of AIDS involve substance abuse or homosexual behavior, but the spread of AIDS among heterosexual teens is also alarmingly high.

Also on the list of preventable STDs are conditions such as gonorrhea, the different kinds of herpes virus, genital warts and chlamydia. These problems can cause painful genital symptoms, such as blisters, itching and burning, as well as more serious effects such as sterility, infertility and life-threatening symptoms.

Often overlooked among the sexual issues that can impact adolescents is homosexuality. With their sexual awakening, a surprising proportion of teens will discover that they are lesbian or gay. Some writers feel that children with a homosexual preference may represent up to four percent of our adolescent population. The inclination toward the same sex in these teenagers is much stronger than in those adolescents who are simply experimenting with homosexuality, which is fairly common. Although homosexuality is not well understood, mental health professionals no longer consider it to be a form of mental illness. Nevertheless, the strain a homosexual orientation puts on a young man or woman is tremendous. And parents who discover what the situation is are faced with a heart-breaking dilemma.

Communication and Safety

The thought of death or injury to one of his or her children is every parent's worst nightmare. The statistics we have just examined about driving, drug and alcohol use, and sex-related tragedies are anything but reassuring. Are parents totally helpless?

No, but neither are they omnipotent. On the negative side, parents must realize that—as we have seen—it's normal for teens to experiment. Unless they chain their youngster to a post in the basement or unless they happen to end up with a complete Straight Arrow, Mom and Dad can't stop experimentation.

On the other hand, research has confirmed what common sense suggests: *the more open the communication with parents, the safer teenagers are.* Says Laura E. Berk in *Infants, Children and Adolescents*, good communication between parents and child is "a powerful preventive of adolescent injury." Teens who can talk freely with—and who get along reasonably well with—their parents may be less likely to engage in risky behaviors. They identify more with their parents' values, are perhaps better informed, and are probably less likely to displace anger against their parents onto their activities outside the home.

Before you start getting all excited and thinking, "If I can just keep the lines of communication open, my kid won't take any chances," think again. There is more to the story, because other studies have reached a conclusion that is both worrisome and reassuring. The worrisome part: research has found that teens who talk candidly with their parents about sex are not less sexually active (though you can bet their parents wish they were!). The reassuring part: these kids are more likely to use birth control, thus reducing the risk of pregnancy and STD.

The message is clear, but it still makes us squirm. You can't control all the behavior of your teenager. You must, of course, maintain reasonable rules and restrictions about things like hours, grades, driving, alcohol and drug use. But you must also do your best to maintain a friendly and open relationship with your adolescent offspring.

In the next two chapters we will discuss strategies for talking with and getting along with your teens. ("Getting along" does not mean a perpetually affectionate and conflict-free coexistence.) These strategies can serve several purposes. First of all, they can help you enjoy your kids—as opposed to having them drive you crazy during your last years living together. In addition to enjoying one another, getting along improves everyone's self-esteem. And a good relationship always makes it easier to handle problems when they do occur.

Finally, a reasonably friendly and open relationship with your kids enhances modeling effects: the kids tend to look up to you more and to identify more with your values. We assume, of course, that you are a good model in the first place. Note that we said good—not perfect—model (remember our lesson on objectivity!).

We'll talk more later about managing teen risk-taking behavior that involves driving, alcohol and drugs, or sex. But at this point one thing should be perfectly clear: the most important reason for you to maintain a good relationship with your teens is their safety.

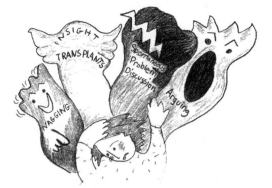

5

The Four Cardinal Sins

W here are you going?"
"Out with the guys."
"What guys? You know it's already 8:30."
"I know."
"Who you going with?"
"Tom, Dick and Harry."
"I'm serious, pal."
"Mike and maybe Bobby."
"Maybe Bobby? Oh, really?! Why does that idiot always
  have to go along? How many times have I told you that
  kid's trouble, but you don't ever want to listen to me, do
  you? Where are you guys going?"
"McDonald's."
"What do you need at McDonald's? We just finished eating
  dinner."
"We're just going to hang out."
"Wonderful. That's how half the trouble starts in this town.
  Kids bumming around with nothing to do. I assume your

homework's done."

"Perfectly, precisely and brilliantly."

"Listen, wise guy, I just asked a simple question."

"I'm outta here."

"You get your majesty back at a decent hour—you hear
me?—or there'll be plenty of trouble around here!"

Ouch!

There are several "tactics" that are so destructive, if used on a regular basis, that we call them the "Four Cardinal Sins." In the above example, our overly conscientious and self-righteous parent just committed all of them:

1. Spontaneous problem discussions
2. Nagging
3. Insight transplants
4. Arguing

There is something seductive or compelling about the Four Cardinal Sins. Actually, these activities don't really deserve the label of "tactics," because they are merely primitive and impulsive emotional responses that occur without much thought. Any parent who reflects seriously on his own behavior will have to admit that The Four Cardinal Sins don't accomplish anything. They do, however, place an adolescent more at risk by irritating the daylights out of him.

The Four Cardinal Sins must be avoided if you are to have any chance at a decent relationship with your child, or any chance at constructively solving problems. It is usually true that in families where there are significant difficulties with teenagers, these four mistakes occur all the time. In the aggravating scene at the front door that you read a moment ago, the parent's poorly-thought-out questions and comments actually *in-creased*—rather than *decreased*—the chances of that teen getting himself into trouble.

If, as a midlife parent, you yourself are doing poorly and you are under too much stress, you may very well be committing the Four Cardinal Sins more often than the average parent, because you are using them to blow off steam. Try to remember that if you are all stressed out, *you* shouldn't be dealing with your teenager unless it's an emergency (a messy room or a ring through the nose is not an emergency). The Four Cardinal Sins are all misguided attempts at dealing with problems, so if you're not supposed to be dealing with your kid at all, try to remind yourself to give up or let go—at least until you're doing better.

The sins that must be avoided at all costs:

1. Spontaneous Problem Discussions

This is a real killer. You see something that needs to be done, so you simply mention it to your kid, right?

Wrong!

Here's a common scene:

"When are you going to start that chemistry paper?"
"What?"
"Your term paper for chemistry?"
"It's not for chemistry."
"Then what's it for?"
"It's for biology and I'll get to it."
"You've been saying that for two weeks."
"I said I'll get to it—get off my back!"
"If I didn't stay on you, you wouldn't do anything."
"If you don't shut up, you'll be doing the @#$% paper
    yourself!"
"Watch it, buddy, I'm warning you."

Here the well-meaning parent sees a problem and, naturally, says something about it. What the parent is saying is perfectly valid and not intended to cause trouble.

The catch? The odds that the adolescent is also motivated to discuss this unpleasant subject at this time are about zero. In fact, spontaneous problem discussions almost always increase irritability and decrease cooperation. The child is almost always doing something else—even if it's only watching TV—and it takes a while to get "psyched" for talking about something unpleasant. You may feel this point is stupid, but it's not. It is a fact of human nature. Chances are you feel the same way about people interrupting you with unpleasant things.

What would you expect the kid to say, "Gee, thanks for reminding me about that darn old term paper. Your concern for my academic welfare is heartwarming!"?

Sometimes spontaneous talks are unavoidable, but in general you need to make an appointment with your adolescent to discuss an important problem. Tell him—short and sweet—what you want to talk about, and agree on a time to get together. Take him out to eat if you want.

This is a better approach:

> "I'm concerned about your grade in biology. When would be a good time for the two of us to talk this over? It won't take very long."

The reaction of some parents to this suggestion, however, is "Give me a break. What am I supposed to do, coddle the kid all his life?! Wouldn't want to interrupt the poor baby while he's watching television now, would we? After all, the poor thing just suffered through two hours of Nintendo while all his homework sat on the kitchen table."

Touchy, aren't we? This type of feeling may be common and understandable, but before talking to an adolescent about something sensitive, you'd better ask yourself if you are just trying to cause trouble or if you are really trying to solve the problem. If you know in your heart that the reaction to your request or statement is going to be negative nine times out of ten, you had better come up with a different approach.

2. Nagging

Nagging can be defined as a set of repetitive, often hostile verbal reminders about something that one person wants to see accomplished. It is usually directed at a second person who does not share the first person's enthusiasm for the project. And, as is the case with the first Cardinal Sin, nagging occurs on the spur of the moment.

Nagging never works well and usually just produces friction. Yet it is a very frequently used parental tactic when Mom or Dad is trying to get a child to do something. The use of nagging brings up a very interesting paradox: why would a parent—being a basically reasonable, intelligent and well-meaning person—use a strategy over and over that has been proven time and again not to work?

There may be two answers. First of all, the parent may not know what else to do. Second, nagging is a spontaneous, poorly thought-out action that comes primarily from emotional frustration. Under conditions of emotional stress, human behavior often becomes much more primitive.

Behind nagging is a psychotic parental delusion—the notion that repetition will make an idea or request sink in. If asking the teen 22 times to clean his room didn't work, maybe the 23rd time will be the charm!

What is the antidote to nagging? First, be sure that what is going to be discussed is important (i.e., not an MBA), and then make an appointment. We repeat: don't open your mouth unless it's absolutely essential, then make arrangements to take the little darling out to dinner or something.

3. Insight Transplants

The third Cardinal Sin often takes the form of a parental lecture. The frustrated mother or father gets hold of his or her offspring and explains the facts of life to him about one thing or another. What the parent is really thinking—or hoping—goes something like this: "I will take this wonderful insight I have learned regarding life, put it into words, and send it through the air waves. It will enter my child's ears and proceed to his brain where it will take root, flower and subsequently generate new and more productive behavior."

This type of thinking—if you really reflect on it—also borders on psychotic delusion. Johnny is getting Ds in his sophomore year of high school. Dad sits him down, explains that this type of behavior will not lead to a .well-paying job, and describes the study habits that made him valedictorian of his class 20 years earlier. Johnny responds by declaring, "Gosh, Dad, that sure makes a lot of sense," and he goes on to achieve all As and Bs during the remainder of his high school career.

That would certainly be nice, but it's not going to happen. Nevertheless, parents attempt Insight Transplants all the time. Once again, the point is not that what the parent is saying is stupid. On the contrary, it probably is very logical; but ironically, saying it accomplishes nothing and often causes irritation.

We often suggest to parents who are inclined to lecture their children that they open their eyes and closely examine the face of their teen during the one-sided talk. Is there a scowl or a snicker there? Are the eyes rolling or is it the Great Stone Face? Many kids, instead of listening intently, are simply thinking, "Here's another repeat of item #43 from Father's Famous Lecture Series. How can I either shut him up or get out of here ASAP?"

We're not saying that giving your children advice is dumb. But if you are thinking about being an advisor, 1) ask yourself how many times you have said the same thing before, 2) pay attention to the response you're getting, and 3) don't get your hopes up that immediate change is forthcoming.

4. Arguing

A psychologist friend of mine once said that the best advice he could give to parents of adolescents was to never argue with their teens. This is excellent advice. The three other Cardinal Sins often give birth to major arguments, which damage relationships further and sometimes even lead to physical encounters.

Surveys of parents which ask Mom and Dad what they find to be the most common and aggravating problems with their adolescents invariably turn up arguing as a major difficulty. Don't forget, however, that it always takes two people to have an argument. You cannot do it by yourself—so don't contribute to it.

Parents often ask, "What are we supposed to do if we don't argue: just keep our mouths shut and let the kids have their way?" Definitely not. When it is essential, you must try to see to it that your children are doing what they are supposed to, but it's very rare for anyone to be argued into submission. Arguing usually results in battle lines being firmly drawn. Each person's ideas become more and more extreme, and sometimes the combatants start saying things they don't even mean. The whole point of the "discussion" becomes to win and, if possible, find some clever way of making your opponent look stupid.

Nothing is really gained from all this scheming. It just produces more conflict or—even if you intimidate your child into submission—smoldering resentment that will cause more problems in the future. It's also likely that whatever you are saying you have said many times before, and you can guarantee that this will not be the time your message gets through.

What are your alternatives? Don't start a conversation that is bound to go nowhere, as our frustrated parent did before at the front door. Consider making an appointment if the matter is really important. And don't insist on having the last word. Let your son or daughter have the last word—provided it isn't horribly abusive, but then make sure she is doing what she should be (see the Major/Minor System in Chapter 12). If you do need to say something, say it directly and succinctly, and then shut up and leave. Don't stick around to counter ridiculous arguments from your teen.

Let's review the Four Cardinal Sins: Spontaneous Problem Discussions, Nagging, Insight Transplants and Arguing. If you surveyed teenagers, you'd probably find that these top their list of obnoxious parental behaviors. That fact by itself, however, does not mean you shouldn't talk. There are plenty of times when some kind of direction—stated once—is necessary.

The real issue here is that the Four Cardinal Sins don't solve anything; but they do ruin relationships and, most importantly, *they compromise your kids' safety by increasing the adolescent's desire to act up*. And for some reason, these Four Sins are addictive, even though they don't do any good. If you do not eliminate them from your playbook, it is highly unlikely that anything else we suggest will do much good.

In summary, then, the basic strategy for dealing with The Four Cardinal Sins is the following:

1. If the problem you want to discuss is an MBA, shut up.
2. If it's important, make an appointment. Go out for dinner or a drive in the car.
3. If the discussion becomes an argument, don't argue. Say instead, "This conversation is stupid, I'm history" and leave.

6

Getting Along

Most parents want to get along with their kids as well as possible. Since you both come from different planets, however, getting along with your teens is a lot easier said than done. As we have seen, maintaining as friendly and open a relationship as you can is important for many reasons. It's more fun. It raises everyone's self-esteem, strengthens kids' identification with their parents, and makes problems easier to resolve. And with the dangers of the Big 3 (driving, drugs and alcohol and sex) constantly lurking in the background, getting along with you makes your adolescents just a little bit safer.

There are several ways of improving how you get along with a teen. None of them is particularly easy, but here are four positive substitutes for the Four Cardinal Sins:

1. Active Listening
2. Talking About Yourself
3. Shared Fun
4. Positive Reinforcement

In healthy relationships, these kinds of interactions probably happen more or less automatically and regularly. If your relationship with your child needs some work, however, and if you think you have the time and energy, here's what you can do.

Active Listening

Active listening is a way of listening and talking to someone sympathetically. The process tries to accomplish two things: 1) to understand what another person is saying and thinking—from his or her point of view; and 2) to communicate back and check that understanding with the person doing the talking. The listener is an active participant in the conversation, rather than some shrink-like being who just sits and nods from time to time.

Active listening is not easy, but it can be mastered. Once you get past the point of feeling artificial, "parrot-like" or too passive, you can sometimes pleasantly knock the kids right off their feet. Active listening should always be used at the beginning of any problem solving discussion.

People who do counseling or psychotherapy have to use active listening when meeting a client for the first time. If they don't, they won't get the critical information they need to help solve problems. Picture this scene: a lady walks into a psychiatrist's office and says, "Doctor, I've been feeling rather depressed lately."

Before she has a chance to continue, the doctor says, "Depression? No big problem. I deal with that all the time and it's one of the most treatable things there is. Why, I'd venture to say that with some antidepressant medication and six to eight weeks of cognitive therapy you'll be feeling much better, and after that we can take a look at..."

This is ridiculous, of course. This doctor is missing the boat in two ways. He is not getting all the information he needs, and he is also not doing anything to build a healthy and cooperative relationship.

The same thing is true in dealing with a child: if you don't listen, you may not get important information you need to know in order to realistically attack a problem. You also undermine the relationship further.

Imagine your 16-year-old son went to a party on Friday night. On Saturday morning he gets up about 10:30 a.m. and comes down to the kitchen where you are reading the paper. No one else is home, and he says, "Well I finally did it. I got high last night for the first time."

How would you respond? Imagine, feeling rather startled and upset, you chose from the following:

"I never want to hear that kind of talk again, young man!"
"Well, fine, you're grounded until further notice."
"Great, so now you're on drugs, huh? Listen, pal, when I
  was a kid..."
"How stupid can you be!? I told you those friends of yours were
  nothing but..."

These, obviously, are not active listening responses (though they certainly are tempting). They shut down the conversation, and the high-powered parent loses a shot at some very important information. What did the boy take? Marijuana, alcohol, PCP? Experimentation may be normal in teens, but what prompted this? Was it really the first time? Why is he telling me this now? (Actually, a teen's telling you something like this obviously implies either a pretty good relationship to start with, or an overwhelming desire on his part to provoke the daylights out of you).

Now let's imagine that you come up with an incredible response—something like this:

The Idiot: "I got high last night for the first time."
You: "Hold the phone. You caught me off guard. You want to tell me
  what happened?"
The Jerk: "You'll get all cranked out of shape."
You: "Well, I can't guarantee I won't be upset or worried, but I'll try
  not to scream."
The Moron: "OK, maybe. Well, ah..., me and these new guys went
  over to Lou's house, and they had some of this pot—you know
  what that is?—he bought, and I'm like, 'Whoa, what's this stuff?'
  and so John told me that it wasn't so bad, so I...(etc., etc...)"
You're Like: "Sounds like you didn't want to look like a wimp with
  these new guys, so you felt sort of pressured."
Your Son: "Yeah, although it wasn't so bad till I threw up. I really

couldn't say I was like really high. I was more like, you know, not feeling too good or something..."

The Partially Relieved One: "You felt sort of embarrassed and it wasn't so great?"

Mark: "I suppose."

You: "You sound a little disappointed."

This conversation is quite different and the teenager is opening up much more. The parent is getting useful and important information (in this case it's more reassuring, though that certainly isn't always true). The parent is also exercising purposeful self-restraint by 1) not killing the conversation, 2) not killing the kid, and 3) knowing how to help the conversation along. In a situation like this, discipline or restrictions may very well follow the conversation; but the point is this: *listening must come first*. It's very hard to deal intelligently with any problem if you don't know what the problem is.

Adolescents can say many things that severely test one's patience, and very often a parent's spontaneous response is not very helpful. What would you say, for example, if your 15-year-old son said something like:

1) "I don't think sex before marriage is so bad."
2) "I think Camels taste a lot better than Winstons."
3) "I'm gonna get my nose pierced—all my friends are doing it."
4) "This family is really boring!"
5) "You know, I think your eating so much is going to kill you."

These kinds of statements can catch you off-guard. If you are going to try to actively listen, remember that your goal is first to try to understand what the other person is thinking and saying, and second, to let him know that you are trying to understand.

How do you do this? There are several different ways that this can be done, and once you get used to them, the whole process can feel quite natural.

Openers

You might start with what are called "openers"—brief comments or questions designed to elicit further information from your child. These can include such statements as:

1) "How's that?" (Sex)
2) "I'm listening." (Smoking)
3) "Let's talk about it—tell me what you're thinking." (Ear Piercing)
4) "Really?" (Joys of Family Living)
5) "Fill me in—so to speak—on what you're thinking."
   (Criticizing Your Eating Habits)

These comments require self-control, and are especially difficult when you are caught off-guard. They may also appear incredibly passive or wimpy to you, but remember that active listening must precede any problem-solving discussion. If discipline or other action is necessary, worry about it after you've gotten the facts.

Questions

An opener can be a question or it can be some other kind of statement, but usually further questions will be necessary. To be effective, questions must not be loaded or judgmental. Here are some bad questions:

1) "Why are you obsessed with sex at your age?"
2) "Why don't you stick with Camel straights and see if you can kill yourself?"
3) "Why on earth would you do a thing like that?!"
4) "So what's your problem today?"
5) "Why do you always hit me with the same old garbage?"

These questions will inspire argument or silence. Here are some better questions that might keep the talk going, as well as elicit more information (be prepared to be accused of sounding like a psychiatrist):

1) "How many of your friends have had sexual relationships?"
2) "So you tried smoking and liked the taste?"

3) "How much does it cost to do something like that?"

4) "Why do you think we never do anything you like?"

5) "How come?"

In print alone, of course, we can't describe the tone of voice that should accompany these questions, but it should be readily apparent that any of the above could be totally ruined by a sarcastic, angry, belittling, condescending or totally smart-alec tone of voice.

Reflecting Feelings

If you are going to tell someone that you think you understand her, it's usually helpful to let her know that you can imagine how she must have felt under the circumstances she's describing. Again, you may be accused of sounding like a shrink, but if you are, just say, "Sorry, but I'm just trying to make sure I understand what you're talking about," or, "Give me a break, I'm doing my best to figure out what's going on!"

Imagine the five conversations above continued. At some point in the discussion, the parent might have an opportunity to say:

1) "You were really embarrassed thinking everyone else knew more about sex than you did."

2) "You're really curious about smoking."

3) "In your bunch of friends you're feeling odd without a nose ring."

4) "Sounds like you feel our family is almost depressing."

5) "You're afraid I won't live to see 50."

Be careful here, because some adolescents don't like to admit or talk about their feelings to you, and even though you may be right on target, they may deny or take offense at what you're saying. As a kind of safeguard, the tone of all of the above statements can be changed somewhat so they come across more as questions. Then it's more like, "Am I right that you felt this way?" The teen can then agree with you, deny or reexplain the feeling. If you are still getting defensive responses every time feelings come up, scratch the feelings part, and stick to a more "intellectual" type of conversation, using just the other active listening tactics.

Checks or Summaries

From time to time during a talk, it is often helpful to check with the teenager whether or not you are "catching her drift" or really getting a good idea of what she's saying. These kinds of comments let you know whether or not you're understanding her correctly, but they also have a second purpose: they tell the adolescent that you're really listening to what she's saying.

Using our five examples again—but changing the order just a bit—the parent's conversation at some point might go like this:

> 2) "What you're saying is that if Dad and I can smoke—and we know it's not good for us—you should be able to as well?"
>
> 3) "Sounds like you think you'll fit in more, and also perhaps look better, if you can get your nose pierced?"
>
> 4) "You're telling me that you think we don't do much as a family, and when we do it's pretty boring to you?"
>
> 5) "You think I don't really care much about my health anymore, and the main reason is what my job has done to me?"
>
> 1) "So in your enlightened opinion, the old fashioned morality about sex is just so much hogwash, and now you and your peabrained friends can make your own rules while nobly striving to impregnate all the females in the western hemisphere?!"

Time out. Did we lose our cool in that last example? Yes. It's very difficult—especially when aggravated—to stay on track when trying to active listen. If you feel you're about to blow it, excuse yourself and come back later for another try.

This type of listening is also an attitude. *Your* attitude, not your child's. It's the attitude of sincerely trying to figure out what someone else is thinking even if you don't agree, or even if it drives you nuts. Who knows, listen and you might learn something new.

Or you might have to lay down the law.

Talking about Yourself

With all this talk about active listening, it's easy to focus too much on your teenager. You can wind up feeling like you're trying to constantly "diagnose" the boy or girl to see if anything's going wrong. Teens quickly pick up on an overly solicitous or overly inquisitive attitude, and then they get defensive. They may also start avoiding you.

One father described his son's behavior as "cave-itis," meaning that the boy spent almost all his time at home in his room. The cause for this withdrawal, it turned out, was that the boy didn't feel it was safe to come out! Every time he showed up, he was "greeted" with statements like, "Is your homework done?" "Where did you get that shirt?" "I think it's about time for a haircut," and "Can you give me a little help around here today?"

A good antidote to this kind of relationship is to spontaneously talk about yourself. Horror of horrors! It's amazing how many parents seem to be almost phobic about discussing their own thoughts, concerns or problems with their children. This reticence is too bad, because many children of all ages would be very interested in hearing what their parents think about their jobs, their friends, about middle age or about something interesting that happened to them that day.

Just so you don't get overly self-conscious, pay attention to two things before you plunge into self-revelation:

1. There can be no hidden message or moral in your story. Perhaps you were hoping that we had just come up with a sneaky way of getting some valuable point across. Sorry. That would only be a subtle version of one of the Four Cardinal Sins—the Insight Transplant routine. The point of your story can only be the inherent interest in the story itself.

2. Pick something interesting. If you just relax and let yourself be spontaneous, it may not be too hard to come up with something. It should be what you'd normally like to talk about anyway. How about:

"You won't believe what my boss said to me today!"
"Do you know I always hated biology?"
"I almost got into a fight in the Jewel parking lot this afternoon."
"When I was a kid, I used to love collecting baseball cards."
"I can't say I'm looking forward to my fortieth birthday."

"When I was your age, I sometimes worried that absolutely no one of the opposite sex was going to like me."

Some parents have trouble with opening up because they feel they don't want to burden their children with their problems, or they feel that—as parents—they are only supposed to be interested in their children. They may also have some kind of distorted idea that their children shouldn't know that Mom or Dad might be unhappy about something. This is the old "Be Cheerful and Keep a Stiff Upper Lip" notion of what a role model should be.

This attitude is almost the same as trying to present oneself as perfect, above it all and able to handle anything. Can you see a problem with a parent coming across this way all the time, and combining this stance with a constant focus on the teen's problems? This kind of "I'm just fine, but you still need a lot of work" idea is wonderful for creating belligerence in youngsters.

Some parents have trouble treating their kids as equals from time to time, even though such treatment might occasionally be appropriate. Consider the possibility that occasionally your kids might be able to active listen to you. Adolescents might even have some good advice, now and then, for Mom or Dad.

Should you tell your kids about the risk-taking behavior you engaged in as a teen? This is a tough question, but here's some advice. By all means don't present yourself to your kids as a former Straight Arrow if you really weren't one. Let the kids in on some of your secrets. That doesn't mean, of course, that you have to tell them every single stunt you pulled. On the other hand, if you have a rotten relationship with your teenage son or daughter, don't tell them anything. They'll simply use it against you or use it to justify their own acting out.

Shared Fun

Find any two people who regularly have fun together and you will find a good relationship. But finding a common activity both you and your teen can enjoy can be harder than finding one for you and your spouse! However, doing something together that you both enjoy is—to a relationship—like water and fertilizer to a plant. This notion may sound corny, but it makes perfect sense. For those having trouble finding something to do with a son or daughter, at the end of the chapter we'll tell you what activity is usually the simplest and best bet.

When "trying" to have fun with your kid, several simple rules must be respected. Ignoring these precepts means certain death.

No problems!

When you're out horsing around together, you are not allowed to discuss anything difficult or controversial. In other words, the long list of all the things you want your child to change about himself or herself must be temporarily abandoned.

Imagine you and your 15-year-old son decided to go fishing. You are slowly floating down the river after having caught a couple of catfish, enjoying the sun and the calm rocking of the boat in the water. The fish remind you that you're hungry, so you mentally check your pockets for lunch money. There's enough—you're a good provider. Will your son be? Not if he keeps performing like he did on that last science test. You'll set him straight. So you blurt out, "I still can't believe you got a D on that biology exam." The fun is over.

One-on-one is better

Don't even try to take the whole family along if you're going out with your adolescent for some fun. It's much easier to get along with someone when there are fewer people to complicate the situation. Also, parents of adolescents report very frequently that one of their biggest problems is sibling rivalry, and you won't have any fun if you are constantly having to keep two kids off each other's back.

In addition, many teenagers, have a nasty habit of not wanting to go out with the family because it isn't cool to be seen like that by your friends. (One 13-year-old girl always sat in the back seat, and then hit the floor whenever she thought she saw someone she knew.) Don't be offended, this is perfectly natural. Going out with only one parent, however, may be a little more tolerable for an adolescent.

Consistency

Doing something enjoyable together on a regular basis is a good way to give a relationship some positive stimulation. Often activities have to be planned in advance, which can provide other benefits. If two people know that they are going to do something pleasant together on the weekend, this knowledge will tend to produce a "backup effect." The idea will help them get along better Monday through Friday.

No martyrdom allowed

Try to avoid doing something that the teen likes and you hate. If you are not having a good time at a rock concert, for example, your feeling ill at ease is likely to show. The two of you may then argue or snipe at one another, and the whole experience may become worse than doing nothing at all. Although it isn't always easy, the two of you want to find something that you can both enjoy at the same time.

The sure thing (?)

Is there anything an adolescent and his middle-aged parent can enjoy together? The closest to a sure thing is going to a movie and then getting something to eat afterward. It's not that difficult to find a movie you can both enjoy, and if you're not getting along too well to begin with, this idea also has the advantage that you don't have to talk to each during the show. Afterward, while you're eating, you can at least discuss the movie a little.

What if your youngster refuses to do anything with you? Try not to act hurt or insulted. Remember that the kid's main job during adolescence is to get ready to leave home for good. Try to be as patient as you can, don't take it personally, and do the best you can with the other tactics for getting along.

Active listening, talking about yourself, shared fun. Aren't these all wonderful ideas? A new relationship in no time! Of course it's not so easy, but neither wishful thinking nor righteous indignation will get you anywhere. If you think you have the energy and time, it's on to the last tactic.

Positive Reinforcement

When you have a bad relationship with anyone, the idea of praising or commending that person for something sounds anywhere from impossible to insane. Yet a compliment is one of the best ways to improve how you get along with an adolescent, provided you do it right.

Positive reinforcement simply means that you let a teenager know when you think she has done something well. You can say something to her while she's actually doing whatever it is you appreciate, or after she has completed the task. It might go something like this:

"Looks like you put a lot of effort into that paper."

"The grass looks real good."

"Thanks for helping me move that stuff into the basement."

"I can't believe how great your room looks!"

"I think you handled that problem with your boyfriend better
    than I would have in your shoes."

There's nothing too tricky about making comments like these, but again there are a few points you need to keep in mind.

Some kids like effusive, elaborate praise and recognition, while others like a more brief, businesslike approach. By the time they are adolescents, more teens will be be in the second category, so it may be best to keep praise short and sweet. Also, if you're not in the habit of expressing appreciation anyway—or if your relationship is pretty bad, you'd better start out small so your statements don't stand out like sore thumbs. Even if it feels a little awkward and embarrassing, though, just try it.

With positive reinforcement, consistency is also important. Consistency can be very difficult, especially when a child irritates you frequently. Some parents have found it's helpful to work a sort of "minicontract" with themselves, in which they agree they will say three to five positive things per day.

You've probably heard the old advice about not criticizing the child but criticizing the behavior? Interestingly, the same rule holds when it comes to positive feedback. It is better to point out what the youngster did right and perhaps elaborate on that, rather than to try to say what a wonderful person the adolescent is. The latter approach comes across as inappropriate and embarrassing.

Finally, don't leave your objectivity behind. Some parents say, "There's nothing good to say about the kid!" This assessment is rarely true. There's a book that's been around for a while called *Catch Them Being Good*. The point is that if you are really paying attention and your attitude is right, you will see lots of things to reinforce.

How Well Do You Get Along?

How much work does your relationship with your adolescent need? Let's take a quick look. Think of three dimensions: talking together, shared fun and liking (not loving). Use the following rating system:

> Excellent
>
> Good
>
> Average
>
> Poor
>
> Rotten

In a relationship rated excellent, you and your teen get along extremely well. You can discuss and resolve problems as well as enjoy just "shooting the breeze"—spontaneously spending time together just talking about whatever comes to mind. You often do enjoyable things together and don't have a lot of trouble finding activities that you both can enjoy. You genuinely like (and love) each other, and look forward to the other person's company.

In an average relationship you can talk, but it's sometimes awkward or hostile. Occasionally you find yourselves talking spontaneously about some interesting subject. Problems are sometimes resolved when you discuss them, but these discussions can also lead to arguments and no resolution. You do a few things together from time to time, but your interests vary and you often can't understand why the other person likes what he does. You find each other pleasant to be with at times, but you also can find each other taxing and irritating.

The bottom of the barrel, according to our scale, is a rotten relationship. Things between the two of you are consistently terrible. You rarely talk, but when you do, you just argue. You tend to take opposite sides on even neutral topics. Aggravating problems are not resolved and continue to simmer. You don't do anything together and generally consider the other person's interests idiotic. Though you may still love each other, you basically find the other person obnoxious.

After evaluating your parent/teen relationship, you may decide you've had enough of this kid and you are just going to Grin and Bear It until he leaves home in a year. On the other hand, you may still feel some hope and—for your own as well as your teen's welfare—you may wish to work on getting along better.

Where Do You Start?

The strategies in this chapter vary in terms of how much control you have and how much cooperation from the teen is required for success. Where a relationship is somewhat strained, start with tactics over which you have more control. Get started with these, then go on to some of the methods that require more help from the adolescent.

First, the Four Cardinal Sins must be avoided; otherwise you might as well not bother with the other tactics. The good news, though, is that the Four Cardinal Sins are under your direct control. You don't need the teenager's help to stop your own nagging or lecturing. The next tactic that you largely control is positive reinforcement. Do it in short bursts— hopefully of enthusiasm—in the beginning. The teen doesn't even have to respond. Next, don't just focus all your attention on your teen. Relax, let your hair down and talk about yourself some. Let the kids know you're human and imperfect and that there's more to you than your job as a parent. All the kids have to do is stick around briefly for your stories.

Then active listening might be used to good effect, but it requires more input from the kids. For a parent, listening in this way takes practice, but it is extremely helpful and it's good for everyone's self-esteem.

If you get this far successfully, you'll be doing pretty well in improving your relationship and getting along. You might as well plunge into shared fun. It will be easier because you'll be communicating much better, and there will be much less chance of unpleasant surprises.

Part III

Problems!

7

Midlife Parent

So the normal adolescent tends to be weird, aggravating and argumentative. He is less talkative and more and more interested in doing things his own way. He likes friends more than family. He knows how the world should be run, but can't seem to keep his room straight or take out the garbage when he's supposed to.

Who's going to help this creature make the transition from childhood to adulthood? That's part of what parents are for. But before we go proposing all kinds of brilliant ideas, and Dos and Don'ts for Mom and Dad, let's take a moment to reflect upon where these older folks are in terms of their own lives.

Midlife! The notion strikes terror into the hearts of some people. If parents are old enough to have teenage sons and daughters, they are old enough to be at this potentially difficult point in their own lives: 35, 40, 45, 50 or beyond. For many adults this age involves the painful realization that they now have more experience than dreams—the exact opposite of adolescent psychology. The parent's mental state might look something like this:

```
┌─────────────────────────┐
│                         │
│                         │
│   Experience            │
│                         │
│                         │
├─────────────────────────┤
│        Dreams           │
└─────────────────────────┘
```

What's more, the realities and experience are certainly not all they were once cracked up to be. The career that once held such great promise may not have produced the desired financial rewards, status or satisfaction. Even for those who are successful, each morning demands getting out of bed for a repeat performance. Others feel a vague longing, after 15 or 20 years at the same job, for something different.

Of all the cherished dreams of childhood and adolescence, perhaps the one that takes the greatest beating with the passage of time involves love and marriage. In recent years the divorce rate has hovered around 50 percent. Large numbers of mothers—and more and more fathers—are single parents. Many of the couples who remain together do so for reasons of finances, children, lifestyle and so on—even if they are not especially happy with their relationship with their spouse. If you add it all up, the odds of experiencing a satisfying marriage may be substantially better than 50 percent *against* you—a far cry from the old "and they lived happily ever after" feeling many people had on the day they got married.

Midlife also brings increasing health problems and a greater consciousness that life won't last forever, what one writer called a sense of "the dark at the end of the tunnel." Mom and Dad's own parents may have died already or may suffer from serious health problems, making these realities even more graphic.

For some people these thoughts are not always conscious, but simply lurk in the back of their minds. But the awareness, for example, that many of your favorite childhood actors, actresses and singers are dead, or that you are now older—rather than younger—than almost all the major, active sports figures, can give you the uneasy feeling that life is more than half over. This realization certainly does not mean that all parents of teens are depressed, but it does mean that—at this point in their lives—parents of adolescents will be experiencing stresses that are regular, sizeable, fairly abundant and predictable.

On top of all this, these midlife parents have to tolerate, get along with, stay in touch with, and sometimes manage a changing adolescent.

How Are You Doing?

How well you handle the normal irritations as well as the bigger problems you encounter with an adolescent will depend a lot on how well you are doing in the first place. Take a moment to evaluate yourself at this point in time. Think of three dimensions: daily stress, usual mood and self-esteem. If you had to rate yourself on a scale from 1 to 10, how would you come out? Imagine a scale that goes like this:

> Life is great (10)
> Things are pretty good (7)
> I'm doing OK (5)
> Things are not so hot (3)
> Life is awful (1)

If you gave yourself a rating of 7 to 10, you feel happy most of the time and generally satisfied with your existence (no one is happy all the time). Your job and relationships with your spouse and important other people can provide stress, but the stress you experience is usually challenging and nothing you can't handle. You normally find your activities rewarding and you have fun on a regular basis. Even though you know you're not perfect, you are also aware that basically you're a decent and competent person, and you know that other people also appreciate these qualities in you.

A parent falling in the 4 to 6 range feels that life is so-so or OK.

Sometimes this parent feels fine about things, at other times not so good. She experiences a fair amount of stress and occasionally is not so sure how to handle it. She can have fun, which may include doing things with other people. Her perception of herself is that she's about average, and she is aware of significant weaknesses in her behavior or personality that bother her.

A rating of 1 to 3 here means that life is the pits. This midlife parent usually feels down and/or burned out. Problems that he has are generally overwhelming and he doesn't feel at all capable of handling them. He doesn't have a lot of fun and tends to avoid spending much time with other people. His self-esteem is low or nonexistent. Often he sees himself as being nobody or totally useless.

In making these ratings try to think as objectively as possible. Often middle-aged adults, when thinking about age and aging, tend to go to extremes. They either joke around all the time or they get excessively morbid. What is the reality of your life right now?

Dreamer Meets Disillusioned

What happens when Dreamer—the young adolescent—meets Disillusioned—the midlife parent? It's hard to imagine a worse combination! These people are supposed to live together, get along and try to resolve problems!? Many adolescents and their parents do get along very well, of course, but there are still some frequent and common problems that parents can run into when their children reach the ages of 13 to 18.

Parents were once adolescents themselves, believe it or not. Almost all adults have fairly vivid memories of what their teenage years were like. When their children reach that same stage of life, Mom and Dad often find that their children's adolescence triggers "old tapes" or memories of some of their own past successes or conflicts. Sometimes parents overidentify with their children's pain and try too hard to help. An overly anxious parent will invariably aggravate a teenager. The parents' constant worrying will produce arguments, misunderstandings and a tremendous amount of domestic conflict.

On the other hand, Mom and Dad may start to remember all the things they did as teenagers that their parents didn't know about. They then begin to worry about what their kids are up to, thus making themselves too suspicious and also, perhaps, too inquisitive—like our parent who committed the Four Cardinal Sins in the front door scene.

Most parents also see their children as reflections of—and on—themselves. It is certainly no fun to feel that your self-esteem is in the hands of someone else, especially if that someone else seems so committed to being different from you. Do I want to take him to our friend's house for dinner when he dresses the way he does?

Children are a reflection on their parents to some extent, but this feeling is often exaggerated. A parent's fear of embarrassment can sometimes lead to attempts at overcontrol. It may help to remember that our children were never really putty in our hands, and that the kids were affected by many other influences in growing up, such as heredity, friends, society, good and bad luck, other adults and so on.

Finally, the relationship between Dreamer and Disillusioned can be strained by something else. By the time a child hits adolescence, the job of parenting him is about 70 percent over. It's definitely getting late. For example, some parents, looking at their 17-year-old son, don't like what they see: strange hair, sloppy clothes, pierced body parts and a sullen attitude. In a state of near panic, the parents attempt "crash courses"—last-ditch attempts to shape up or modify the kid before he escapes the house for good.

These attempts often involve long lectures, scoldings or arguments. Sometimes the kid is unnecessarily dragged off to a shrink. These efforts are rarely successful. It's almost as if the parents see themselves as manufacturers of some kind. The child is their product. He's getting close to the end of the assembly line, but he's not at all what he's supposed to be. Better get in there quick and do something!

Emotional Dumping

There are plenty of times when parents of adolescents must take charge, intervene and do something assertive in their kids' interests—whether the teens like the idea or not. More about that later. Our focus here, however, is on unnecessary parental intrusions—intrusions that are based more on *parental stress* than on *problem severity*. Parents who are too stressed out themselves are notorious for repeatedly using the Four Cardinal Sins on their children's MBAs.

Earlier we asked you how you were doing in terms of daily stress, general mood and self-esteem. Believe it or not, the first step in getting along with any adolescent is to make sure that you're OK. If earlier you rated yourself as not doing too well, it might be helpful if you attended to your own problems first. After you get yourself back on track, you can worry again about your child.

If you are not doing well, there are several reasons why taking care of yourself first might be a good idea—or why it may, in fact, be essential. One reason for taking care of yourself first: if you are really stressed-out, you will not be able to talk about any problems without getting very upset. You will just be too sore. You will probably do more damage to your relationships with others, and it's not very likely you'll solve any problems.

A second reason for taking care of yourself is quite simple: why should you spend another hour of your life feeling unnecessary pain if there's something you can do about it?

Finally, if you are in bad shape, perhaps the biggest problem you will experience is one that is invisible. It is called "displacement." Displacement is kind of a fancy term for what is otherwise known as "emotional dumping." It refers to our uncanny tendency to transfer feelings from one situation to another—without really being aware of what we are doing. A father who has just been chewed out by his boss at work, for example, may return home and yell at his wife because their three-year-old left her tricycle in the driveway.

The odd thing about emotional dumping, however, is that while Dad is yelling at his wife, he will actually feel and believe that the bike is the problem. The real source of his being so stressed-out—what happened at work—will in a way be "unconscious" to him, or more or less forgotten. His wife, of course, will also believe that the tricycle is the problem, unless she gets more information about what happened to him at work.

Displacement, therefore, actually involves two things: 1) an exaggeration of the seriousness of a problem, and 2) a focus on the wrong problem. How does this apply to handling a problem with an adolescent? If you are really doing poorly yourself, you will tend to have an exaggerated view of the seriousness of your teen's problems. Everything will seem like a big deal, even though it may not be. You might, for example, start thinking of a girl who really is average or competent as a walking catastrophe. You may also get extremely upset about minor problems, such as a messy room or a lot of time spent on the phone.

Perhaps worst of all, you might not realize that the biggest source of your distress is you, the midlifer, and not your child. If your teenager has some sense that displacement is going on—that she is basically OK and you are overreacting to her minor offenses—she will begin to resent you more and more.

War!

Kids can dump or displace their negative feelings onto their parents, just as parents can onto the kids. If this goes on for too long—and especially if it's going both ways—it can produce a more or less permanent state of war.

A number of years ago, in a book called *Games People Play*, Eric Berne described some of the goofy ways that people interact with each other, and he labeled these unproductive transactions "games." A game always had some superficial plausibility to it, according to Berne, but underneath the "player" was really trying to accomplish something else— often some hidden, self-serving and emotional objective.

Berne used somewhat odd, humorous titles for his games, such as "Kick Me" and "Why Does This Always Happen to Me?!" What was probably the most common of these games he called "Now I've Got You, You Son-of-a-Bitch!" In this game one person repeatedly catches another doing something wrong, and then proceeds to have an enjoyable temper tantrum—scolding, blasting or lecturing his target for the horrible transgression.

The plausible part of "Now I've Got You" is that something was done that was wrong, and it might need to be pointed out or corrected. The hidden part of the game, though, is the emotional satisfaction the chief player gets out of venting his spleen and having a well-justified, much deserved, self-righteous temper tantrum.

Of all the negative emotions—anxiety, guilt, depression and anger—

anger is somewhat unique. No one ever enjoys feeling anxious or guilty. A few people can enjoy feeling a little depressed, especially when they feel sorry for themselves. But lots of people can enjoy being angry—not all the time necessarily, but it can be quite satisfying now and then to blow up.

In fact, repeat this pattern for a while and it's possible to "get high" on anger and eventually get addicted to it. And what better creature to give a parent their regular anger "fix" than some obnoxious adolescent, especially if the kid also is playing his own version of "Now I've Got You."

So if you've totally had it, and want to become an accomplished "Now I've Got You" player rather than just your average crabby mother or father, here are some suggestions:

1. Think of your adolescent as a total problem child, even though he's really average or competent.
2. Always find something to criticize the teen for, no matter how small (a sign of success here is that your son always leaves the room when you enter).
3. Constantly evaluate and diagnose the child; keep a sharp look out for any signs of something that is either wrong or just plain irritating.
4. Voice all your worries about him to him. Be consistent.
5. If you have had an especially rotten day, get loaded at night, see the teen as the source of all your problems, then have a royal tantrum.
6. Constantly work on maintaining the exalted mental state of Righteous Indignation.
7. Use—and reuse—the "Famous Lecture Series," including those old favorites:

"When I was a kid..."
"If it weren't for you..."
"When are you going to learn..."
"No one does anything around here but me..."
"If you'd just listened to me in the first place..."
There are also other tactics that frustrated parents have found

successful for ruining relationships with their adolescent children. If the kid's not around, you can go check his room for drugs, birth control devices, or just plain messiness. During conversations you can use clever arguments and interruptions to make his thinking look stupid, as well as listen in on his phone conversations or try to find a diary to get more ammunition.

Blaming one's physical ailments on the adolescent has always been an effective way of inducing guilt, and you are assured of an aggressive, angry response whenever you ask the little devil about his homework in the middle of his favorite TV show. Finally, a vital part of any consistent, warlike program should always be grilling the child about simple requests, such as use of the car, where he's going, whom he'll be with, if he's dressed properly, and so on. Be sure to repeat yourself and respect the nine-question minimum.

Seriously, if you feel you might be getting into a state of war with your teenager, take our simple Anger Addiction Test. Answer these three questions:

1. Am I getting quite angry at this child on a regular basis?
2. Am I going out of my way to find things to get mad about?
3. Do I enjoy blowing up at this kid?

Although it may be hard, try to be as honest as you can. If you answered "Yes" to these questions, you are probably addicted to anger and you are either in—or about to be in—a state of war. That means you are deluding yourself that your "corrective efforts" are geared toward helping the child shape up. Your real underlying motive is to play "Now I've Got You."

What to Do

If you are in bad shape, or you are contributing constantly to a State of War, something needs to be done. How should you proceed? It depends on the issues and there are no simple answers, but here are a few things to think about.

Perhaps it would be a good idea to get yourself into counseling or psychotherapy. Lots of people have done it, and often with very good results. Research has proven over and over that depression, anxiety and a whole host of other problems can be significantly altered through counseling with the right kind of professional. Sometimes certain kinds of medications can also be useful.

If you do find a counselor, make sure you like him or her. If you don't like the person and don't feel comfortable after two or three sessions, go find somebody else. Remember that you have a right to shop around.

You say you don't need any help from a shrink and you'd rather go it alone? These days there are quite a few helpful books that have to do with managing stress and other psychological problems. Perhaps you can talk to a friend or professional to find one that might be good for you. There is a time limit here, though. Give yourself two months, and if you don't feel any better by then, find a professional therapist to talk to.

Does your marriage need some work? Don't they all? No one's relationship with his or her spouse is perfect, but if this is one of the problems that is bothering you a lot, it might be a good idea to give it some thought.

It's quite easy to say you will go into marital counseling, but it's a totally different matter to actually do something about it. For starters, men frequently don't care for the process very much, and they can be quite resistant to the idea. Also, men and women usually have very different thoughts about what they expect out of their marriage. Women are normally much more interested in things like closeness, companionship, open communication and orientation toward family. (More women than men, for example, will read this book.) Women, therefore, are usually the ones who initiate discussions about problems, as well as attempts at marital therapy.

Whether you are the husband or the wife in this situation, if you are thinking about marital counseling, here are some Do's and Don't's to remember:

- Try to pick your counselor together or, if one person is
  more reluctant to go along, let the reluctant one choose.
- Go in to see the counselor together the first time if you can.
- Before as well as during any counseling, try to listen
  respectfully to your spouse's point of view, even if you
  don't agree.

Research has shown that marital counseling can be quite helpful—if you can get both parties involved.

Perhaps the major cause of your stress is not your teenager or your marriage, but your job. At this point in their lives, many parents—mothers and fathers—have been working on the same job for many years. Changing occupations or positions is certainly not easy, but ask yourself several questions. Do you spend a lot of time complaining to others about your work? Do you consistently feel overloaded and unappreciated when you're there? What do you think of your boss, and how do you get along with her? How about coworkers? How do you feel on Sunday nights—or each morning when you wake up and realize it's a work day?

How about the physical side of your life? You're no spring chicken! What kind of shape are you in? You may be tired of hearing this, but it is very helpful to get regular, vigorous physical exercise three to four times per week, especially if you are routinely feeling anxious, angry or otherwise stressed-out. *A regular exercise regime for yourself is one of the best things you can do for your kids.* If you don't take your frustrations out on the racquetball court, you may very well take them out on your son or daughter. Do you have some physical problem that needs attention, or are you avoiding that physical exam because you are afraid of what the doctor will say? Check the problem out; don't let the worry fester in the back of your mind and make you even more irritable.

Pass the Buck? Maybe

Finally, taking care of yourself may mean that you must temporarily pass the buck to your spouse when it comes to dealing with your troublesome teenager. This temporary renunciation of responsibility will make you feel guilty, but keep in mind that—if you are in terrible emotional shape—you would probably make things worse by trying to do something.

You may also feel that your spouse may not be as conscientious as you would be in trying to handle a problem. It's too bad you feel that way, but unless there is an emergency, it's time for you to avoid getting involved. Some people say that's why God made two parents, so if one is out of commission, the other can take over.

What if you don't have a spouse anymore, you simply have an "ex"?

See if your ex can help out with the child, and if he or she can't, try to find a counselor for both you and your teen. If you do try to work out something with your ex, it may require laying to rest a lot of old hostilities, so make sure you're really prepared to make an honest effort.

If you do finally get your act together and start feeling better, what is the first thing you should do with your adolescent? Nothing! Go back and reevaluate your situation to see if you still think there is major cause for concern. MBAs are aggravating even if you're in good shape, but they're still MBAs.

If you do think you're in pretty good shape—emotionally and physically—and you are concerned about your adolescent, just what exactly are you going to do? First you must take some time to think over exactly what your role should be.

8

Understanding Your Job

When something about your teenager is bothering you, stop and think before doing anything. Shooting from the hip can cause a lot of trouble. You need to ask yourself two questions:

1. Does this problem need my attention or intervention?
2. If it does, how involved should I get?

Four Possible Roles

There are basically four roles a parent can consider when responding to a problem. They vary in their level of intrusiveness. From least intrusive to most invasive they are:

1. Observer

2. Advisor

3. Negotiator

4. Director

As an Observer you stay out of the trouble and merely watch what happens. Observing is an appropriate role for the MBA type of problem as well as other issues which you want to let the teen handle himself. You may get involved if the situation worsens. As an Advisor you express your opinion to your child, but not more than once, and you are ready to accept the possibility that the teen may not take your advice. If you choose to be a Negotiator, you are going to sit down, talk the problem over, and try to come to some resolution. Finally, if you take on the role of Director, you are going to impose a solution—whether the teenager likes it or not—when you feel a problem is serious and your adolescent is not handling it well.

How do you decide which role to take? Let's assume you are in good emotional shape and are not a serious displacement candidate. After that consideration is taken care of, several others should be kept in mind.

1. All in all, how well is your child functioning?

In general, the better your child is doing, the less you need to be involved, and the more you can stick with observer or advisor roles. As the kids get older, they should also be growing more independent and competent, so you will give a 17-year-old more leeway on many issues than a 13-year-old. Kids who are having a lot of trouble, however, will usually need more involvement for serious problems. Intervention in these situations does not mean, of course, large, regular doses of the Four Cardinal Sins!

2. How good is your relationship?

If you get along well with your teenager, any kind of intervention is easier. The child will accept advice from you more easily, and it is also easier to talk things over when negotiation is necessary. You won't need to take charge as much. A bad relationship, however, may mean you have to be a director more often; negotiating and advice may become almost ridiculous or impossible. If your rapport with the teen is really bad, make sure you don't open your mouth unless you have a very good reason, and watch out for displacement.

3. How serious is the problem?

With less serious difficulties, you should be sticking more with the less intrusive alternatives. Keep in mind that your level of aggravation about a problem is not always the measure of the real seriousness of the problem. Examples? Six earrings on only one ear, jeans with holes, messy rooms, sibling rivalry, occasionally eating junk food, and other MBAs. On the other hand, eating disorders, anxiety, depression, ADD and conduct disorder are serious, and justify concern as well as more parental intervention.

In trying to decide what role to play, your general philosophy should be to stay out of the kids' problems unless it is necessary for you to get involved. The teens are at the point in their lives where they are supposed to be handling things more and more on their own, and inappropriate attempts at direction from you can cause useless irritation and conflict.

Some people refer to this issue as "problem ownership." Whose problem is it, really, and do you absolutely have to make it yours? If you have a teen who's generally doing well academically, for example, but who is currently getting an F in Spanish because he hates the teacher for some weird reason, perhaps you can legitimately not get involved. Or you have an average child who is dragging his feet in looking for a job, or wearing some kind of weird T-shirt to school. Maybe your "help" isn't needed and you can let the big, bad world instruct your youngster.

Getting Mixed Up

A lot of trouble can occur when a parent decides to take one role and his child assumes that another role would be more appropriate. Sixteen-year-old Michelle, for example, plans to go on a double date Saturday night. She, a girlfriend and two guys will go by train from a suburb to downtown Chicago to hear a concert in the evening. The four kids will return together afterwards on a train that departs from the big city at 11:30 p.m. In the middle of the week, however, the plans change. It turns out that neither of the guys can go. Michelle informs her father that she and her girlfriend will go alone. Dad says, "No way," and a royal argument ensues.

Part of the problem here is the role each of the combatants thinks Dad should take. Michelle thinks Dad should be only an observer—or at most an advisor. Dad, on the other hand, thinks he should be a director if necessary.

<u>Teen's Choice</u>   vs.   <u>Parent's Choice</u>

√	Observer
	Advisor
	Negotiator
Director	√

A lot of arguments take place when this unspoken difference of opinion occurs. These "discussions" are very confusing because two things—the actual problem and the parental role—are being talked about at the same time.

What to do? If you're the parent, make up your mind what role is correct in the first place and then stick with it. Tell your teen what role you are going to take. If you have chosen a less intrusive role, such as advisor or observer, stay with it even if you get anxious or angry.

Imagine your son, for example, is a junior in high school. He has just purchased a CD that consists of some of the most repulsive rap "music" you have ever heard. You decide, however, to shut your mouth and merely be an observer. (Actually, you don't even want to listen to the stuff.) One night, though, you and he start discussing his musical preferences. You express the opinion that his CD choices bear no resemblance to music and that they are obscene. He says your music is sappy and has no real social message. One thing leads to another and you forbid him to play his junk in your house anymore.

You made a mistake. Anger has pushed you from observer to an inappropriate director role.

By the way, who was right in our other example, Michelle or Dad? The answer is Dad. His choosing the director role was what he should have done. Two 16-year-old girls are not going downtown to the big city and back by themselves on a Saturday night.

9

Observer

As an observer, you are really not intervening at all in your adolescent's life. You are trusting your child to handle things. Your daughter, for example, has a new friend that you don't particularly care for, but she's generally a competent kid and you respect her opinion. Or your son is getting to bed somewhat later than he used to. You're worried that it may affect him during the day, but so far he seems OK. You can keep a watchful eye on what's happening. If worse comes to worse, you may proceed to an advisor or negotiator role. Or you may still want to let the adolescent handle things himself.

Being in the observer role does not rule out sympathetic listening. This is often an excellent idea for basically competent kids and nonessential problems, such as a diet, a friend you don't like, or a temporary drop in a grade. While listening, remember the notion of "letting go" and don't give unwanted advice. Perhaps while lending a friendly ear you'll learn something reassuring. Then again, maybe you won't. But if you do come upon some disturbing information, take some time to think about it before doing something more assertive. Remember that anger and anxiety can push parents into roles that may not be right for the situation.

There may be many times when you find yourself worried or irritated, but—if you really think about it—you still feel your involvement is not a good idea. Maybe your 16-year-old son is eating junk food after school and you think he should have fruit. Perhaps you don't like the way your daughter talks to one of her friends, or she always studies with the radio on.

The Awful Scale

In these situations you can try to more aggressively let go by using the "Grin and Bear It" approach. To do this you'll need to use what we call the "Awful Scale." Here you create a kind of subjective/objective scale that ranges from 0 to 100, and use it to rate the "awfulness" of different events that might happen in your life. In other words, you are rating how miserable different things might make you. Something rated 0, for example, would not bother you at all. A rating of 15 would be a minor hassle, while a rating of 85 would indicate an extremely taxing situation. An event qualifying for a score of 100 would be something that would make you permanently miserable.

Once you have the general idea of the Awful Scale, you need to practice rating different incidents or circumstances. What would you rate a flat tire on your car at the end of a long work day? Some people say 10, some 20 or 30. What if you broke your right arm, and you are right handed? 30 or 40? What if your house burned down? Most parents say 60 or 70. What if your spouse died? Some people say, "It depends on the day," but most people put a loss like this in the 90 to 95 category.

Do you know what almost all parents consider to be the worst thing that could happen to them? The death of a child. People will say "That would be 130," or "I can't even imagine it." But most parents agree that it would be as close to 100 as anything can get.

With this perspective in mind we return to some of the actual problems that parents are concerned with in their children. Your male son comes home sporting a new, purple, dangling earring and carrying a progress report with two F's on it. What would you rate that? Many parents say something like, "Why that little creep! That's an 85 or 90 easy!"

We now try to gently point out to Mom and Dad that the rating for the earring and the grades is only 10 or 15 points away from the rating for the death of the child, which obviously can't make any sense! What is needed is another long look at how bad the problem really is. What usually happens is that—upon further review—the original rating will not stand as it was. Realistically, the true "awfulness" is most often quite a bit less than what was first thought or felt.

So Mom and Dad are asked to "re-rate" whatever it is that is bothering them. Reevaluation certainly doesn't mean that everything becomes a 0, but it does mean that, on the scale from 0 to 100, an earring probably merits a rating of 0.06 and the grades perhaps 4.2.

What kinds of problems and in what kinds of situations might you consider only observing? You should stay away from the MBAs, unless you already have a reasonable and effective way of handling these minor problems. For kids who are for the most part pretty capable, you might stay out of concerns such as bedtime, dating, work, use of money and selection of friends.

What if you feel you are being objective about the problem, but you still can't stand what's happening, or you think you really should do something? The next least intrusive role is that of Advisor.

10

Advisor

In the world of business a consultant is a person who is hired to give advice. There are two conditions to the contract. First, the consultant will be paid for his work. Second, the person who receives the advice has the right to accept or reject it. Except for the pay, consultant is the role we are talking about in this chapter for parents of adolescents.

"I wish you'd cut your hair shorter," "Please clean your room this weekend," "If you want my opinion, I think you're trying to push your boyfriend around too much," and "I think it would be a good idea if you got your homework done before we leave" are all potentially legitimate consultant statements. They are attempts to give advice, and with fairly good relationships the parent/consultant stands a good chance of at least being heard. As an advisor, however, you are still only a consultant to the child, which means you are not using power and the adolescent has the right to reject your advice.

If your advice or request doesn't change the situation, you have two alternatives (neither alternative is to repeat your "advice" over and over). With small problems, you may just go back to being an observer and perhaps the "Grin and Bear It" approach.

If, on the other hand, you feel the issue is more important, you may want to go on to the next parent role, that of negotiator.

Now, if you are going to consider trying to be an advisor to your child, don't shoot from the hip. There are a few considerations you should think over before you open your mouth.

You probably weren't hired for the job. If you are going to give your daughter some friendly counsel, remember that it was your idea to do this and not hers. If she asks for your opinion, fine. But if she doesn't, be careful. For example:

> "Better comb your hair before you leave."
> "What?"
> "You heard me—you can't go to school looking like that."
> "Who asked you, anyway?"
> "Watch that tone of voice, young lady."
> "For your information, this is how they wear it nowadays!"
> "This may be the new age, but you look like a witch, and I'm not
>   letting you out of the house like that!"
> "Dad, it's my hair—not yours!"

The teen has a point—this is MBA territory. She's also getting mad about the unsolicited consultation, especially from a male of the species.

As we have mentioned, before you say anything, make up your mind what role you're taking. In the above example, Dad gave absolutely no thought to this issue at all. Some of the biggest conflicts between teenagers and their parents occur because the parent feels one role is appropriate (e.g., director), and the child feels another role is correct (e.g., observer or advisor). If advising only is appropriate, try to stick with that tactic, even if you get angry. The hair-related conversation between Dad and daughter might continue in two different ways. In the first scenario, because he gets mad, Dad forgets that he shouldn't be telling his 17-year-old daughter what her hair style should be:

> "It may be your hair, young lady, but I'm your father!"
> "And an internationally known hair stylist, no doubt!"
> "That's it, smart alec! Upstairs! Read my lips—comb! Or you're not
>   setting foot out of this house!"

Bad ending. Dad's anger at his daughter is pushing him into an inappropriate director role. Now let's imagine instead that the conversation goes something like this:

"Listen, your hair really looks sloppy."
"Dad, what do you know about hair styles for teenage girls?"
"Enough to know it's your funeral."
"I like it like this."
"Fine, be my guest."

Here Dad is not happy, but he is not getting into something he should stay out of. Kids do have some weird hair styles. Remember, parents and teens are from different planets.

On the other hand, if directing is appropriate, stick with that approach and don't be intimidated by the child's anger. In the next example, Dad tries a little friendly advice first:

"I'm leaving—see you later."
"Don't be too late, honey. What time you coming home?"
"Two or three."
"Not! Curfew's 12."
"Dad, my friends will laugh at me. I am 16!"
"And I'm 42. Be back at 12."
"Oh, for pete's sake!" (Exit Miss Grump)

Here Dad is taking charge, and he should. Hours for a 16-year-old are not subject to the whim of the child.

Unwanted advice is a problem by itself, but when the unasked-for wisdom comes out of the blue, things are doubly rough. The response is very likely to be irritation and absolutely no receptiveness to whatever you are trying to say.

How can you get around this if you're just dying to say something? Here are several ways. First, see if you can get "hired" as a consultant to your teen, or at least warn her that some discussion may be coming. You might say something like, "You mind if sometime we talk about these kids you've been with the last couple of weeks?"

Second, if you think consulting is the appropriate role for you with this child and this problem, clarify out loud before any discussion that you only want to talk, that you may or may not give any advice, and that any advice you may give can be used or not—as your youngster sees fit. Make up your mind that you will only be a consultant. This commitment will help you not feel like a wimp as a parent, and it will also help you to not jump into a heavier role if the teenager makes you angry. Clarifying your role will also make your adolescent less defensive, since she will be assured that the final decision is up to her.

Third, in any discussion about a problem, you should active listen first. Unfortunately, it may be true that few teens are going to want to listen to your opinions much in the first place. You increase your chances of being listened to, however, by having the patience to hear your children out before you speak.

Do Something Weird!

Your adolescents aren't the only ones who can do strange things. You can, too! If you are about to dispense a potentially unpopular piece of advice, why not do it in some unusual way?

One of the tactics that many parents have found helpful is to go out somewhere special to talk things over. You can actually take the teen out to dinner. This strange maneuver accomplishes several things. It is fun, or at least it can be. It also says to the adolescent that you are serious enough to do something very unusual. Rather than trying to communicate your concern by yelling or nagging, you underline it in a pleasant—but perhaps equally explicit—manner.

Another idea is to write out your thoughts and give a note to your son or daughter. Parents often forget that the sound of their voice can be very irritating, especially when they are worried. A brief note is sometimes more helpful. Some parents have even drawn simple cartoons to try to get their point across. Now that's weird!

When giving advice, you also want to be realistic and accept the fact that, even though your ideas may be perfectly valid (since parents rarely give stupid advice), your inspirational notions are not likely to be acted upon. You may be in the curious—but very common—position of having something quite reasonable to say that will make absoultely no difference as far as the behavior of your teenager is concerned. Most teens would have a hard time maintaining their own self-respect if they followed *all* of their parents' advice.

Being an advisor, then, may not work. When their advice fails, many frustrated parents take their pleasant request and repeat it 350 or 400 times, tack on an excerpt from their Famous Lecture Series, or beg, plead, threaten, nag or yell. These are just different versions of the Four Cardinal Sins; you'll blow off some steam, but you won't accomplish anything. If advice doesn't work and you still feel the issue is important, you may want to try negotiating as a next step.

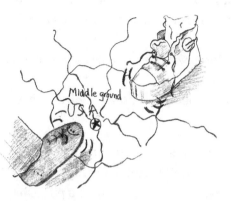

11

Negotiator

The beginning of an attempt at negotiation might go something like this: "We've got a problem here and I'd like to talk it over with you sometime." What you are doing here is recognizing that the child is older now, and that he should have more say about many of the things that he does. Negotiating is also a statement that you feel it is important to be involved, because you think the problem is serious or it affects more family members than just the one adolescent. But you are saying that—up to a point—you are willing to bargain or make a deal.

Although negotiating doesn't have to be anything horribly fancy, it is critical that you follow certain minimal guidelines:

1. Agree to negotiate

You can't just plunge in. Remember the rule outlawing attempts at spontaneous problem-solving discussions, and never insist on an immediate talk unless a total emergency exists. Also, don't bring up the idea of having a talk when you are already pretty cranked out of shape about something. Chances are your teen will go nuclear on you, you won't get anywhere, and it will be just that much harder to bring the issue up again.

How do you broach the subject of making a deal with the kids? Imagine these possibilities:

> "When's a good time for you to talk with me about the leftover food in your room? It's starting to smell up there."
> "You may not be too thrilled by this suggestion, but sometime in the next couple of days I want to sit down with you and talk about college."
> "I can't say I care for your new work schedule too much. Can we go over it together sometime?"
> "We gotta talk about your smoking. Not now, but tell me when's good."

In responding to these opening comments, kids may actually attempt to talk about the problem prematurely. When they are caught off guard like this, however, it is unlikely that you are going to have a profitable pow-wow. It is more likely that—in the interests of their budding independence—the youngsters are simply going to try to get you off their backs as quickly as possible. They can do this in two ways. The first is to try to minimize your worries and make light of the problem:

> "What's the big deal?"
> "Oh, Mom."
> "Just chill out, will ya? I'll take care of it."
> "Now, don't start bugging me about that again."

You, however, have already thought it over and have decided the problem was important, or you wouldn't have brought it up, right? So you respond to these comments by telling the teen that you don't want to discuss the issue right away, but that you do feel that it is important. When is a good time for her? Don't get suckered into talking about the problem with an uncooperative adolescent.

The second way the teen may try to get rid of you is to attempt to provoke a fight:

> "Why don't you just mind your own affairs instead of running the whole world? And stay out of my room in the first place!"

"Did I pick where you went to college? Just butt out."

"Why are you always harping at me? I don't see where my work schedule is any of your business. Do I tell you when to show up at that dump you work at?"

"You smoked when you were a kid. Better be careful—you're the one living in the glass house, lady!"

When confronted with responses like these, don't get sidetracked and stumble stupidly into one or more of the Four Cardinal Sins. You are being baited. Keep in mind what your major goal is here (it's not murder). Your objective is only to make an appointment with the youngster to talk. If she refuses to talk, and you still feel the problem is important, you will be going on to the director role.

2. Pick a good place and time to talk

Go to a quiet room, take her out somewhere, or even go to dinner. Often a long ride in the car is helpful (you don't have to look directly at each other). It's great if you can plan something enjoyable to do after the discussion, but this idea doesn't always work. Make sure there won't be interruptions from other family members or any possibility of phone calls.

3. Define the problem clearly to start with

Assuming that you've survived the process so far, your next goal is to define the problem (then you will try to bargain). Here you have a bit of a difficulty. You want to listen to your child to begin with, but *you're* the one who first brought up the problem. The best solution to this dilemma is for you to say what the problem is very briefly, then ask for her thoughts. Don't go rattling on and getting all excited. If you keep trying to talk to your kids like that you'll never get anywhere with anything! How many times have I already said that you can't do that!! Lectures don't work!!! I don't know what it's going to take for you as a parent to get it through your head that this kind of thing...

Oops. The Four Cardinal Sins are very seductive. Where were we? The teen is talking first and you are using active listening. Give her five to ten minutes, longer usually isn't necessary. Don't interrupt, roll your eyes or make faces like she's an idiot. Simply listening and not arguing does not have to imply that you agree with everything the adolescent is saying.

You may not like what you hear. Try to keep your cool, but if you find yourself really upset after the teen has talked, say something like, "Listen, a lot of what you said is new to me and I need some time to think it over. Give me a day to get used to all this, and then maybe we can sit down and we'll try to finish it."

If you're not too upset, ask the child to not interrupt you while you take five or ten minutes to explain your side of things. Stay calm and try not to accuse or blame. Remember, if the issue is something like a messy room, loud music or appearance, the adolescent may feel—correctly— that the issue is not much of a problem.

4. Let's make a deal

Assuming you've gotten through the earlier negotiation phases alive and with the problem clarified, you must now come up with a solution. Actually, some of the time you may not need a solution, because you learned that the thing was not as big a deal as you thought. But usually you won't be this lucky.

To bargain or make a deal, don't get too pushy about your own ideas—even if you feel they're just brilliant. Try to get the teen to make suggestions first and give them careful consideration. You might start the solution-oriented part of the negotiation by saying something like:

> "Well, it's obvious we don't agree, but that doesn't mean we can't come up with some compromise. What do you think?"
> "Tell me what you think would be fair to you and everybody else."
> "What kind of arrangement do you think would work here?"

The sign of a good bargain is that there is something in it for everyone, but everyone has to give up a little something, too. The best solution is one that the teen devises that also helps you feel better. If you can't agree with your child's initial proposal, support the good parts of his idea and suggest some modifications.

Here are some examples of possible bargains:

1. Loud music. Dad agrees to buy Mark headphones for the stereo if Mark will promise to wear them—and not use his large speakers—whenever anyone else is home.

2. Phone. Melissa can talk on the phone as much as she wants as long as her grades don't drop below a C average and as long as she pays the amount over $50 a month on phone bills .

3. Smoking. Mom and Dad agree to stop nagging 18-year-old Tom about his smoking, as long as he no longer smokes in the house.

4. Hair. Parents will pay for Jim's haircut as long as the mop is not left more than two inches below his collar.

What if the teen doesn't want to suggest anything, becomes belligerent or feels there's no problem? You have a choice. You can go back to the observer role (forget giving more advice and shut up). You can grin-and-bear-it (cultivate and refine your skill for tolerating nonessential differences). Or you can move on to taking charge.

If you are able to come up with a solution, it's often helpful to write it down. Some people even sign it like a contract. Though the kids often feel this technique is stupid, try to write the agreement anyway. This small exercise helps you remember what you said and it makes the agreement feel more solid.

If your agreement works well, some brief, friendly positive reinforcement would be in order. For example:

"I think our little deal is working well so far."
"You're keeping your part of our bargain about college so far.
 Do you think your Dad and I are?"
"You seem OK with the new work schedule. Is that true?"
"I don't know about you, but I think—after three weeks of no
 arguments—that we may have solved that smoking problem."

If the deal doesn't work, don't have a fit. Go back to the drawing board, hang on to the good parts of your arrangement, and see if you can agree on the necessary changes. Follow the same basic negotiation format described above.

With good relationships, negotiating is obviously easier than with lousy ones. On the other hand, try to keep in mind that if the relationship is not very good in the first place (and the problems are not emergencies), you should spend perhaps a month or more working on how you get along before tackling any issues.

Also, since problem kids present multiple problems, be sure to stick with one problem at a time. Although a lot of things may irritate you, you certainly can't solve them all at once, and mentioning more than one at a time to a teenager is going to feel like pure, malicious mudslinging.

Just as with the previous parental roles, observing and advising, negotiating doesn't always work. Kids can refuse to talk with you. Attempts at talking can turn into screaming matches. Agreements can be made, but not followed up on. What do you do if negotiating fails? Try it again! Lots of times you'll succeed if you persevere.

But what if you still feel you're not getting anywhere? Take a deep breath and go on to the next chapter.

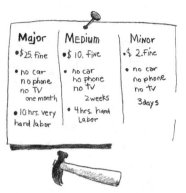

12

Director I:
The Major/Minor System

For many parents of adolescents there are times when no amount of consulting or negotiating is going to do any good. Things have gone too far and problems have gotten too serious. When the situation gets to this point, it is time for Mom and/or Dad to draw the line.

Taking a stand isn't easy. For many parents the idea of trying to tell their adolescents what to do—or of trying to force them to do it—brings up images of ferocious retaliation. The bad news is that teens can and will manipulate and fight back. The good news is that there are only six ways they can do this and *we now know what they are*. If the couple or single parent is ready, these maneuvers can be managed.

If you feel it is time to take charge regarding something in the life of your teenage youngster, you have two choices:

1. The Major/Minor System
2. Evaluation and Counseling

Both of these approaches require clear thinking, emotional self-control and, usually, lots of hard work.

The Major/Minor System

When a problem is serious enough (a 16-year-old smoking in her bedroom) or interferes directly with your life (an 18-year-old's loud music), you have a definite right to become a director and force a solution. If the child has been so uncooperative that advice and negotiations have been useless, the use of power here is perfectly legitimate. But make sure your invasion of the teen's life is not just a camouflaged attempt at waging war.

How do you become a director? First, if both parents are living at home, sit down together, define the problem, and decide exactly how the two of you are going to take a stand on a particular issue. Also, look at the chapter on testing and manipulation, predict what types of testing you'll be likely to get from this child, and prepare to handle them.

Next you give a written warning. The warning is a message to your teen that certain behavior is unacceptable, and if it doesn't change within a certain time, you will institute consequences. Your warning is better written than spoken, because the child has learned to dismiss your words or argue with you consistently, so there is no way of having a productive conversation. So remain silent and don't attempt the impossible: talking. It's "actions are louder than words" time.

Here is an example of a warning note to a 16-year-old girl. Her parents feel that she is an average kind of teen and her relationship with them is OK most of the time:

> *Dear Mary,*
>
> *Smoking in your bedroom is something we can no longer tolerate. Talking about it with you has been useless.*
>
> *If you stop smoking in the house from now on, we will take you and a friend out for dinner on Dec. 5, or we will help you arrange some other outing of your choice. If you do not stop, as of Dec. 5, your phone privileges at home will be removed until such time as you do stop.*
>
> *Love,*
> *Mom and Dad*

No more talking or nagging. It is absolutely critical that you shut up at this point. Your next step will be doing something, not words.

If the child responds positively, there is nothing wrong with rewarding her with a dinner, special use of the car, trip, CD, outing with a friend, or whatever. A reward is a friendly sign and helps prevent war. The size of the reward can be proportional to the size of the problem.

What if she doesn't respond? Now it's time for action using the Major/Minor System. To begin, you classify a problem as a "big deal" or "little deal." Actually, you could have three or four classifications if you wanted. You might consider something like staying out overnight a big deal, or a Major Offense, and leaving your tools out a Minor one. Cutting a class at school might be a Medium Offense, but three cuts or more would be a Major.

You then decide what consequences will follow for Major Offenses, Minor Offenses and in between. When the misbehavior occurs, you institute the consequence without yelling, lecturing or playing "Now I've Got You!"

> *A guaranteed law of adolescent psychology is this: repeatedly engaging in one or more of the Four Cardinal Sins will always obliterate the effectiveness of any consequence or punishment.*

Parents often wonder just what kind of power or influence they still have over to their teens. It's true that it's harder to come up with power over adolescents; little kids you can drag to their rooms. When your children are older, however, you may still have two kinds of power. One kind is based on your relationship with the youngster; the other is based on the fact that you still control certain amenities that your teenager enjoys.

Relationship power is based on the fact that, unless things have totally gone to pot, your kids basically don't want to hurt you and they do want to please you. Long ago you were a powerful person in your child's eyes. To her, it seemed, you could do almost anything. You also totally controlled your young child's fate for a while. In addition to this kind of respect, relationship power is also based on the pleasant experiences, mutual affection and "bonding" you and your youngster have shared.

In good relationships, respect, liking and love are still active. They may not be totally gone even in bad ones. Relationship power is one of your primary assets when you are acting as an advisor, negotiator or even director. If you regularly engage in arguing, nagging, lectures and yelling, however, you throw whatever leverage you may have here out the window.

Control of amenities is a more primitive kind of power that parents are sometimes reluctant to use. Here your authority is reinforced by the fact that you still control—to varying degrees—many of the material conveniences your child enjoys in this world. You have the right to withdraw these conveniences—believe it or not—as a consequence of improper behavior. What kinds of amenities, you ask? Money in the form of allowances, loans and outright doles; transportation, as in chauffeuring 13-to-15-year-olds and the use of your car by 16-to-18-year-olds; food, laundry service, phone, TV, electricity and toothpaste. The kinds of things you yourself pay for when you go out of town, rent a car and stay at a hotel. You provide these things without even thinking, and while adolescents in many other countries of the world only dream of these pleasantries, our kids take them for granted.

When using the Major/Minor System you are making a deal with your adolescent. It goes like this: "I'll continue to provide these services as long as you behave yourself."

In addition to temporary removal of selected amenities, things like grounding or chores can also be used with the Major/Minor System. However, looking at the list of possible consequences, you can see that some require more cooperative kids in order to be used. With problem kids and bad relationships, it's better to use things that you have more control over, such as fines (from allowance), car use or rides, phone (it can be locked or restricted electronically), or TV's (they can even be removed).

A three category (Major/Medium/Minor) system might look something like this:

MAJOR CATEGORY
Offenses: out all night, physical violence, drinking, party without permission at home with no parents.
Consequence: $25 fine, no TV one month, no phone or

car one month, 10-hour project or chore, grounding for two weeks (can't leave home except for work or school).

MEDIUM CATEGORY
Offenses: behavioral trouble at school, smoking by 13-to 15-year-olds, friends at home without permission.
Consequence: $10 fine, no TV two weeks, no phone for two weeks, four-hour chore, or one-week grounding.

MINOR CATEGORY
Offenses: leaving your tools out, leaving house unlocked, forgetting to feed dog in morning.
Consequence: $1 or $2 fine, no TV for three days, no phone for three days, or two-day grounding.

One of the easiest applications of the Major/Minor System involves the problem of chores. We use what we call the "Docking System." The Docking System works best when the child has either an allowance or regular money from a job. Suppose there is a problem with not feeding the dog, dirty dishes left around the house, not getting laundry down to the washer, or not taking out the garbage, even though these jobs have been clearly defined. The Four Cardinal Sins have not worked (surprise!), nor has advice or negotiating.

The frustrated parent informs the adolescent that she has some good news and some bad news. For example, the good news is that if the garbage is not taken out, the parent will do it herself! The bad news is that she will charge for this service, and each time she has to do it, it will cost so much in cash or so much docked off the allowance. That's it.

If the Four Cardinal Sins are avoided, one of two things will happen. The kids will shape up and begin to do their chores better, or the parent will do the work and get paid on a regular basis. At least then Mom won't have to feel life is so unfair.

Negotiating the Major/Minor System

In some situations, where both the child and the parent-teen relationships aren't so difficult, negotiating and directing can be more or less combined.

Let's assume you have already set up the Major/Minor System and an offense has occurred. It may work well to let the teenager pick his own consequence from the list. If he refuses to pick or delays, you pick and impose. In some families, it's a good idea to have the child negotiate the possible consequences with you right from the beginning.

When setting up the Major/Minor System—and especially when imposing consequences—be prepared for certain predictable statements from your kids:

1. "This is stupid."
2. "I don't care what you do to me."
3. "My friends think you guys are weird."
4. "How come you don't treat anyone else around here like this?"

Don't pay any attention to these comments, but also don't smirk or act superior when the kids make them. Ninety percent of the adolescents who say "I don't care" do care. Just be quiet, do what you have to do, and be prepared for more testing and manipulation.

If the Major/Minor System doesn't work, you just can't seem to shut up, or you feel totally powerless, it may be time for professional evaluation and counseling.

13

Director II:
Evaluation and Counseling

There's no law that says that you, as the parent of one or more adolescents, must be able to handle all problems yourself. There are times when seeking professional advice might not just be a very good idea, it might be essential; there are certain problems that you should not attempt to handle on your own. Here are some of them.

Anxiety Disorders

In some ways it may seem that anxiety and adolescence are synonymous, since many unfortunate adolescents experience extremely large doses of anxiety that make their lives miserable. Anxiety disorders are characterized by an excessive fear of something, and that something varies depending on the type of disorder. Anxiety disorders also devastate self-esteem—as one's anxiety level goes up, self-esteem goes down. Unlike children, teenagers who experience these problems usually know that their anxiety is excessive. Unfortunately, this knowledge often makes them feel embarrassed and stupid. It's not surprising, therefore, that these teens usually don't like to talk about anxiety disorders.

Anxiety disorders tend to run in families, are usually more common in girls, and often start during early adolescence. Recent studies indicate that these painful conditions may be much more common than we have realized. To be diagnosed as an anxiety disorder, the problem must have been going on for some time, usually for more than six months.

With what is called "generalized anxiety disorder" the teenager worries about a number of different things, from performance at school to the possibility of nuclear war to being on time. The child cannot control these worries, which may impair concentration and cause excessive fatigue, restlessness, irritability and difficulty sleeping. The prevalence rate for generalized anxiety disorder is approximately three percent.

With "social anxiety disorder" (or social phobia) the core fear is fear of embarrassment in social situations. The adolescent has an excessive worry—that can sometimes lead to panic—of looking stupid in situations such as public speaking. The teen may also avoid activities like eating in public, for fear others will see his hands shake, or talking to new people, for fear his voice will sound shaky. When these situations are unavoidable, the affected teen's physical distress is considerable and can involve blushing, sweating, tremors and diarrhea. The estimated prevalence of this kind of social anxiety ranges from three percent to 13 percent. It is unclear if this condition is more common in boys or in girls.

About four percent of children and younger adolescents experience "separation anxiety disorder," which is characterized by an unusually strong fear of leaving home or of being separated from one's family or caretakers. Teens who have this problem often worry about their parents being killed. They may have trouble going to school in the morning or going to sleep by themselves at night.

A final kind of anxiety that has received much more attention in recent years is obsessive-compulsive disorder. Affecting both sexes equally, it usually begins in adolescence or early adulthood and may affect as much as two percent of the population. OCD, as it is called, involves unrealistic but obsessive worries that constantly intrude upon the child's mind. The most common thoughts involve fear of germs or contamination, an excessive need for order, and recurrent hostile or sexual images. Often these thoughts are dealt with through compulsions such as repeated hand washing or checking and rechecking locks. These compulsions can begin to take up an amazing amount of time each day.

The bad news is that anxiety problems in adolescence are fairly common. The good news is that these disorders can be successfully treated, often with a combination of education, psychotherapy and medication.

Depression

Depression can also make a teen's life miserable. Depression involves a persistent mood of sadness or dejection and—like the anxiety disorders—is usually accompanied by low self-esteem. It is common for depressive problems to be accompanied by "biological signs," which include difficulties with eating, sleeping and energy level. Children and adolescents do not observe or describe depression in themselves well, and it is important to keep in mind that this disorder may appear more as a major case of irritability and as an inability to enjoy oneself.

In what is known as "dysthymic disorder," the adolescent feels either down in the dumps or irritable most of the time for at least one year. These kids don't appear to have fun like they used to. They can have difficulty concentrating and generally feel hopeless and self-critical. Dysthymic disorder, which will occur at some time or other to approximately six percent of the population, is two to three times more common in females. It is hard to say what the exact prevalence is in adolescents, because the disorder can begin in childhood, adolescence or early adulthood.

Dysthymia can sometimes lead to what is known as "major depressive disorder." While dysthymic disorder occurs most of the day, more days than not, for a period of at least one year, major depressive disorder involves feeling terribly depressed or irritable all the time for at least two weeks straight. During this time the teen seems to be interested in nothing. He may lose a significant amount of weight, sleep poorly and be either agitated or excessively fatigued. Indecisiveness, feelings of worthlessness, and suicidal ideas or thoughts about death are also common.

Depressive disorders are quite treatable with a combination of psychotherapy and medication. Many of the newer antidepressants can produce remarkable effects, and "cognitive therapy," which teaches clients more realistic ways of looking at themselves and at life, can also help a lot with self-esteem.

Attention Deficit Disorder

Attention Deficit Disorder (ADD) has received a good amount of attention itself recently. Also referred to as Attention Deficit/Hyperactivity Disorder (ADHD), it probably affects about three to five percent of our adolescents. It has a hereditary link (it is not caused by bad parenting) and is perhaps two to three times more common in boys. ADD does not start suddenly when a child becomes an adolescent. It is there from the beginning and often starts causing trouble when the child is just a toddler. ADD is also not outgrown. About 80 percent or more of our ADD teens will go on to be ADD adults.

The core symptom of ADD is, of course, a difficulty concentrating that is not caused by another psychological disorder (such as anxiety or depression). In children and adolescents there are two kinds of ADD: ADD with hyperactivity (what is now called the "Combined" type) and ADD without hyperactivity (what is now called the "Primarily Inattentive" type). In ADD with hyperactivity the concentration problem is accompanied by two other symptoms: a lot of motor activity and a lot of impulsive behavior. The child may have difficulty sitting still and is always on the go. He may also repeatedly blurt things out in class without raising his hand or push another kid down when he gets angry.

ADD teens in this first category also show characteristics such as emotional overarousal, silliness and bossiness in social situations, difficulty following rules, difficulty waiting for something they want, general disorganization and incredible forgetfulness. Some people claim that all children are like that, but ADD kids show these signs more often, more intensely and at an inappropriate age, i.e., they act as if they were three or four years younger than they really are.

One factor that has complicated the diagnosis of ADD with hyperactivity in adolescents is that many of these kids are moving around less by the time they get to be teenagers. They are, in other words, less "hyper," but they are still inattentive and emotionally "wired." In the past people used to think ADD would be outgrown, because the most obvious symptom at the time, hyperactivity, often diminished in adolescence.

In ADD without hyperactivity, a major concentration problem exists, but the child may have an average or even placid temperament.

These kids don't run around too much, get too excited, or try to push others around, though they may still sometimes be too impulsive. They do, however, have a difficult time in school and never seem to finish anything. They can be amazingly forgetful, their thinking sluggish, and their disorganization can drive their parents crazy.

An interesting aspect of ADD without hyperactivity is that many of these children are girls. There are many adolescent ADD girls who have spent their lives being disorganized, underachieving in school and being accused of having little motivation. And they didn't receive appropriate assistance primarily because they didn't cause enough trouble (like many ADD boys do) to call attention to themselves.

Attention Deficit Disorder doesn't always appear by itself. In adolescence as many as 40 to 50 percent of ADD kids may also qualify for a diagnosis of conduct disorder (see below). This ADD/CD teen is usually a risk-taker par excellence. Another group of ADD kids—30 to 40 percent—may have learning disabilities, which can cause special problems with certain tasks (like reading) or certain subject areas (like math or foreign language), even though these adolescents have average intelligence.

ADD can usually be managed with what is called "multimodal treatment": a combination of education about ADD, parent training in behavior management, counseling, appropriate school interventions and medication. Approximately 80 percent of ADD teenagers will have a good response to one stimulant medication or another. And, contrary to popular myth, they may need to take the medication throughout their teen years and into adulthood.

Conduct Disorder

The term, "conduct disorder" (CD) is the modern psychological euphemism for what used to be called juvenile delinquency. Onset can be as early as six years of age, but conduct disorder rarely starts after 16. This child's behavior is characterized by a repeated violation of the rights of other people and by disregard of age-appropriate norms or rules. CD children are often bullies who get into frequent fights. They can be physically cruel to other people, as well as to animals. They may steal directly from someone, force another person into sexual activity, set fires or destroy property.

If their child is behaving like this on a regular basis, many parents find themselves wondering if the kid has any conscience at all. On the other hand, some parents of CD children have impaired conscience development themselves. It is true that conduct-disordered adolescents are less capable of sympathy or compassion for others. If they do show remorse, it is often faked in order to avoid punishment. CD teens will often see the intentions of others as hostile—when in fact they are not—and then will respond with aggressive behavior. Conduct-disordered adolescents usually have an exterior of defiance or toughness, and the real nature of their self-esteem is a matter of controversy. Recent studies incidate that these kids may actually "suffer" from self-esteem that is unrealistically high!

Keep in mind that these troublesome behaviors must be persistent, not isolated examples, for us to worry about true conduct disorder. In any one year, perhaps one-third or more of high school males will engage in risk-taking that involves shoplifting, vandalism or fighting.

Some people think that the prevalence of CD has increased in recent years and is also higher in urban locations. Some studies have shown that for persons under 18 years old, six to 16 percent of males and two to nine percent of females may qualify for CD. The good news is that the majority of these kids will no longer behave this way in adulthood. On the other hand, a large enough proportion will go on to "graduate" to Antisocial Personality Disorder as adults. This diagnosis exists in approximately three percent of adult males and one percent of adult females.

Although it is common for most teens to experiment with drugs and alcohol during their adolescent years, the incidence of substance abuse in the conduct-disordered population is much greater than average. It is also more likely to persist into adulthood.

Related to—and overlapping with—conduct disorder is "oppositional defiant disorder" (ODD), which is somewhat less serious. It involves persistent patterns of negative and hostile behavior that are characterized by defiant and oppositional reactions toward parents and, later, toward other authority figures. Oppositional kids just can't seem to do what you want them to. They argue a lot, lose their tempers, seem to go out of their way to annoy others, and frequently blame everyone else for their own mistakes. Unlike conduct-disordered children, however, ODD teens are not as aggressive towards others or as destructive.

This pattern of behavior emerges at least by early adolescence; most of the time it starts at home. In young children ODD involves boys more than girls, but in the teen years the sex ratio may be equal. ODD also overlaps with ADD, and it is often a precursor of conduct disorder.

In part because of the very definition of their diagnoses, conduct disorder and oppositional defiant adolescents are very difficult to treat. They don't take well to therapists (who are authority figures) and they don't accept much responsibility for their actions. If ADD or depression coexist with either CD or ODD, and if the attention deficit or depression can be treated, the prognosis is better. The more aggression there is, the worse the prognosis.

One of the most important prognostic indicators for conduct disorder is family stability and consistency of discipline. CD kids can get you into a State of War faster than you can think. The Four Cardinal Sins must be avoided like the plague, and misbehavior must be managed as clearly, routinely and unemotionally as possible. With regard to professional assistance, parents should keep in mind that even if the teen refuses to get involved and see a therapist, Mom and Dad may still benefit from going themselves and learning how to best manage the difficult situation. This is no small task with CD and ODD teenagers, who are often among the most obnoxious of human beings!

Eating Disorders

Eating disorders have also drawn more attention in recent years. These tormenting conditions affect many adolescent girls. Eating disorders crush self-esteem, so affected teenagers rarely talk about their difficulties openly. The two most common problems are anorexia and bulimia.

Anorexia, which affects girls 90 percent of the time, usually starts during the teen years. It is more common in industrialized countries where the ideal of feminine thinness and the extensive availabilty of junk food often clash. Many writers feel that the estimate that one percent of the adolescent population percentage is affected is too low, or at least that there are many more young girls who are borderline anorexics.

During adolescence 90 to 95 percent of girls will diet at some time or another. Anorexia, however, involves the persistent inability—or refusal—to maintain an appropriate body weight. An anorexic girl, in fact, maintains an intense fear of gaining weight, even though her body weight is already low. An anorexic teen cannot see her body as it really is, and she often sees fat where there isn't any. Many girls who have starved themselves for long enough will stop having their periods. The long-term mortality rate for anorexia is approximately 10 percent, resulting from starvation, suicide or electrolyte imbalances.

With bulimia, which usually begins in late adolescence or early adulthood, the adolescent engages in periodic, secret episodes of binge eating. The amount of food consumed during a binge is often incredible, and it usually involves sweet, high-calorie foods. Most often a binge lasts two hours or less, and it is then followed by "purging." Usually accomplished by induced vomiting (or occasionally done with laxatives), purging reduces both physical discomfort and also the fear of gaining weight. Bulimics, therefore, are often able to maintain a normal weight, but at a high price to their physical and psychological well-being.

Both anorexia and bulimia are very difficult—but not impossible—to treat. The earlier they are diagnosed, the better the prognosis. Some young women also seem to alternate between—or combine—the two disorders. Group treatment has been found helpful, especially in dealing with the shame and self-hatred that often accompanies an eating disorder. Medications have also helped when there is an accompanying mood disorder. There is some indication that some antidepressant medications may also help the hunger-satiation mechanism in the brain function more normally.

Divorce-Related Problems

Divorce can affect children in a number of ways, not all of which, of course, are bad. One of the most difficult is the loss of the parent who leaves the house—usually the father. Although the harm done is usually worse the younger the child is, teens can also be profoundly affected. They often have had to endure the daily trauma of the pre-divorce marital conflict, and in these situations may feel some relief from the separation of their parents. If they have gotten along best, however, with the parent who leaves the house, and if they don't get along with the one remaining, their daily existence can become agonizing.

Another divorce related problem for adolescents is the difficulty they have in "blended" families. Unfortunately, when there is a remarriage and adolescents are involved, "blended" is often a euphemism for "nothing but trouble." The fact of the matter is teens don't blend as well as younger children. This situation is usually aggravated the longer the time has been between the divorce and the second marriage. Many adolescents have an extremely difficult time accepting a new step-parent, and some, in fact, never do. Even worse, some new couples are convinced that a teenager in their home is deliberately trying to break up their new marriage.

In many situations this belief is not far from the truth. Sometimes parents are well-advised to not remarry until their kids are grown and out of the house. What many parents don't see—behind their child's constant irritability and lack of cooperation—is the pain the youngster feels and the child's sense of alienation from both biological parents, as well as from the new parent.

Sexual Abuse

The problem of sexual abuse of children has finally begun to receive the attention it should. It's hard to imagine a more offensive subject. Although estimates of the prevalence of the problem vary widely, many experts believe that by the time a girl is 18, at least one out of three will have been the victim of rape, incest or molestation. The vast majority of the victims are girls, and the vast majority of the perpetrators are males. The trauma to the victim depends upon many factors, including the nature of the assault, the degree of force used, whether the offender was unknown or familiar, the amount of pain involved, the length of time the abuse went on, and the extent to which intimidation was used to maintain secrecy.

Making matters worse is the conclusion of some researchers that three-fourths of parents who have good reason to suspect that sexual abuse is occurring, or has occurred, still do not report it. People do not like to look at or talk about this subject, and confronting it is always traumatic for everyone involved.

The effects of sexual abuse are multiple and often serious. Physical troubles can include chronic pelvic pain, asthma, digestive difficulties, stomach aches, pseudo-seizures, aggravated PMS and generalized physical complaints. Psychological difficulties can involve depression, increased suicidal risk, bulimia, substance abuse and sexual disorders.

Children who have been recently abused may show changes in their normal behavior, including sleep disturbances, drop in appetite, childlike behaviors and exaggerated fears. Some girls may run away from home (especially if incest is involved), while others may not want to go out of the house. Some kids may show a sudden interest in sex or get involved in precocious sexual activity.

Long-term effects of sexual abuse often include problems with trust and intimacy, lowered self-esteem, suppressed rage and a tendency to choose partners who are degrading or abusive themselves. Girls who are victims of incest are often caught between feeling angry about what happened on the one hand, and—surprisingly—feeling guilty and responsible for it on the other, even though this second notion makes no apparent sense. These young women have more difficulty trusting authority figures. After all, they may have been betrayed by one of the people closest to them.

Abuse can make a girl's life unending misery. Professional intervention is necessary, and should be done with a therapist who knows how to handle this kind of problem. Most often—since most victims are female—the most effective therapist will also be a female. Group therapy is strongly recommended by many experts, but many feel that individual sessions are more productive in the beginning of treatment.

Finding a Therapist

The list of problems in this chapter certainly does not include all the psychological problems that adolescents can run into, only some of the more common ones. Other emotional difficulties teens experience can result from psychosis (such as schizophrenia), sexual or gender problems, physical abuse and manic-depressive illness. A good rule of thumb is: if you as a parent have been persistently worried for longer than six months about the possibility of a psychological problem in your son or daughter, you have waited too long. Find someone you trust and get an opinion.

Unfortunately, counselors vary a lot in their approaches and personalities, so you may need to shop around. Getting an initial referral from a friend, doctor or local mental health center may be a good way to start. Don't use the yellow pages first unless you have no other recourse. Call several counselors, briefly describe the situation, and see how you like them over the phone. If these people can't give you a few minutes on the phone, forget them.

When discussing the possibility of counseling with an adolescent, never say, "You need help," or "We're going to get you some help." The word "help" is a sure way to turn anyone off. After all, no teen wants to see a shrink in the first place. Instead, you have a couple of other choices for bringing the subject up, depending on what kind of relationship you have with the teen.

If your relationship isn't so hot, you might say "We're obviously doing a lousy job around here of working out our problems ourselves, so I think we'll see a professional of some sort and get their opinion about what to do." Don't argue about it, just set up the appointment.

If you are primarily concerned about your teenager—whatever your relationship is like—you had best be honest. "I'm worried about how you're feeling. Lately you don't seem to be yourself at all—too down, no fun, sleeping too much and much more irritable. I'm going to ask you to talk to somebody, and probably your Mom and I will too."

Sooner or later, most kids will go to visit a therapist. If the child refuses, you might want to go yourself first and ask the counselor what to do, though it is preferable with teenagers for the child to be seen before the parents. If the teen continues to refuse, you might use the Major/Minor System. For example, "You won't use the car again until you see the counselor at least for the evaluation."

One doctor who often referred people to other professionals suggested a good rule of thumb for selecting a counselor: remember that you are the consumer with the power of choice, and if you have seen someone three times and still don't like him or her, go find someone else.

Hospitalization may need to be considered if the problem is serious enough, and especially if you worry about your child hurting herself. Suicidal threats should always be taken seriously. The rate of teen suicide has increased in recent decades; the most vulnerable adolescents tend to be behaviorally-disturbed males who also abuse alcohol and drugs, depressed females and ambitious but socially isolated perfectionists. The risk is always greater where there is a family history of suicide and/or a previous suicidal attempt or gesture by the child. Danger signs for suicide include the following:

- suicidal threats
- recent loss: family member, pet, boyfriend or girlfriend
- a sense of hopelessness
- loss of interest and/or energy
- preoccupation with death
- social withdrawal
- family disruption: divorce, illness, geographical moves
- giving away valuable possessions

Unfortunately, suicide has become a leading cause of death among teens. These suicides are not usually impulsive; before any self-destructive action is carried out, the teen has usually given it a fair amount of thought.

Not Living Together

Parents have a "rulebook" in their heads that says family members are supposed to like one another, get along and stay together—at least until the kids are grown. Unfortunately, it doesn't always work out like that. Sometimes the teenager is simply too unruly and uncooperative. Sometimes parent/teen chemistry, for some strange reason, is simply rotten, even though both people seem to be doing well on their own.

If and when it comes time to seriously consider not living with their adolescent anymore, parents always feel an acute sense of failure. But as they say in the "Tough Love" program, parents are people, too, with limited resources, and there's no future in blaming yourself for everything that went wrong in the past. The kids, after all, weren't really putty in your hands, and if everything didn't turn out the way you wanted it to, there were certainly many different reasons.

Unless the child himself chooses to leave (at an appropriate age, of course), there are a few alternatives for parents who have concluded they shouldn't live with their teenager anymore. These options involve parents in the director role, and they are not easy to carry out.

Where bad parent/teen chemistry is the main issue and the adolescent in question still gets along well with other adults, some families have tried to negotiate living arrangements with other relatives or, more rarely, with friends. Maybe old Uncle Joe in Michigan's Upper Peninsula needs a little company. Negotiating should be used here as well as it can be with the adolescent and the other family, so that house rules, money and other living arrangements are made perfectly clear.

When living at home is intolerable, though, moving in with another family is not usually a realistic alternative. A second possibility is a boarding school, military school or other treatment facility where kids can stay. Two big problems here: finding a good one and paying for it. Contact a school or local mental health center to get possibilities, and be sure to visit any place before considering it.

A final alternative applies to "late" (age 18 and older) adolescents only: kick the teen out of the house. This advice may sound terrible; fortunately, this drastic action isn't often needed. Booting a child out is also more emotionally difficult for everyone than residential placement, but under really trying circumstances taking this important step may actually be in the best interests of both parents and adolescent. By this time the "child" is really an adult, and he will have to be responsible—come hell or high water—for his own problems.

How do you kick a person out of his own house? You don't do it on the spur of the moment during a fight or argument, unless, perhaps, there has been physical violence. What is sometimes done is a version of the Major/Minor System, where the consequence of poor behavior is having to leave home for good.

You might write a note—or sometimes a lawyer writes the first note—saying something like this:

Dear Joe,

We are having too much difficulty getting along around here. For the next month, we are going to expect the following from you: not coming home after one o'clock any night, no abusive language, no stealing other people's money, and $50 per month rent.

If you cannot hold to these rules, we will ask you to leave the house, since you are now 19 years old. You will be given one month to prepare for this after we give you notice. We will do our best to be unprovocative and reasonable during this time.

Your Parents

If the young person can stick to the rules, fine. If there is a Major infraction, or if his behavior simply does not change at all, then he is given notice. Some "kids" will get mad at the letter, tear it up and screw up right away. They are then given notice. A parent's chances of shaping a kid up with just a letter aren't too good in the first place.

What if the difficult son or daughter won't leave? You get an attorney who writes a letter to your young adult informing him that he is of age and has been asked to leave, and that refusing to do so will be regarded as trespassing. It's no fun—in fact, it's horrible for Mom and Dad—but it works. It's your house, after all, and you have a right to protect your belongings, other children at home for whom you are responsible, and yourselves. What if the "kid" won't leave by the time stated in the letter? Your attorney can instruct you about how the courts and the police can remove *anyone* who is illegally in your house.

14

Managing Risk Taking

One of the most basic and powerful of all animal instincts is parental motivation to protect the young. Parents can accomplish amazing and—sometimes ferocious—feats when their children are endangered.

Most of the time, of course, your children are not in danger, but that doesn't mean you don't think about it. Every parent has worried thousands and thousands of times about her children getting hurt. And the statistics we saw before regarding driving, drug and alcohol use, and sexual activity are anything but reassuring.

Parents need to realize that normal adolescents are going to take some risks. And—as much as you might like to—you can't lock your kid in his bedroom and have him escorted to and from school by the police every day. Like it or not, 100 percent control is not possible. What you want to do is to make sure you have taken reasonable and not horribly restrictive steps for preventing injury to your kids. Then you have to cross your fingers and trust the youngsters.

There is a big difference between worry and preparation. Worrying may certainly lead to realistic planning, but good plans only need to be thought out and made once. Worry tends to go on and on and on, however, even long after good planning is finished. In other words, you may have taken perfectly good steps for preventing adolescent injury, but still find yourself worrying like crazy. There's nothing unusual about that.

In this chapter we'll discuss some ideas for preventing injury due to driving, drug or alcohol use, and sexual activity. We'll also discuss some ways of dealing with trouble if it should occur. There is nothing sacred about these suggestions, but many parents have found them useful. Keep in mind that your best preventive strategy is maintaining as friendly and open a relationship as you can with your teenager.

While you're struggling to stay in touch, consider these other suggestions. Some of them should be implemented before the kids hit their teenage years and some after. You may come up with other ideas that may be equally useful. Remember, though, that no matter what you have done and how much you have prepared, you are still going to worry about injury to your children. As long as you are taking reasonable steps for prevention of injury, the fact that you are still worrying does *not* have to mean any of the following:

1. Your preparation is inadequate.
2. You have to talk, nag or lecture more.
3. The kid's doing something wrong.
4. The danger is great.

Worrying is part of being a parent—and it's your problem, not your child's. Most adolescents take some chances. Unless you resign from parenthood, that means you're a gambler too.

Driving: Prevention

1. Model good driving habits for your kids from the time they are little. Avoid speeding, tailgating, forgetting the seat belt and drinking and driving.

2. In addition to the training received at school, each child should drive a total of 1,000 miles with her parents before getting her license. Parents should be certain that this practice includes all kinds of circumstances, such as driving in residential areas and on expressways, as well as in good and bad weather. You can make an outing of the practice session

and perhaps have some fun together. The teen keeps track of the miles logged and you get a feel for how competent she is behind the wheel.

3. Have your adolescent pay part or all of his insurance. And before he can start driving, he must have six months' worth of insurance payments in the bank. He can't drive without a parent—even if he has his license—until that money is saved. Then he pays you one month at a time for the insurance.

4. If your adolescent qualifies for the good student insurance discount (usually 25 percent), that amount is taken off what she has to pay for her insurance. She earned it.

5. Teens should pay for their own gas. Don't give them your credit card.

6. Without being haughty, explain to your kids that their use of your car, other than for necessities like school, is a privilege. It's your car and you are letting them use it; they don't have an inherent right to your automobile.

7. If you agree to allow a competent adolescent to get his own car, he foots the bill. Make sure House Rules about issues like grades and hours are clear.

8. Mom and Dad must agree with each other about rules for car use. Kids love to play you off against each other. If you do get into an argument about something, *finish the discussion* and come up with an agreement. Don't try to do this negotiation in front of the kids unless the two of you are extremely adept at marital bargaining.

9. Your policy will be zero tolerance for drinking and driving. If he has one beer, he can't drive. If your adolescent has had something to drink, he or she must find a designated driver, call a cab or call you for a ride. If the teen calls under these circumstances, make sure not to berate him. No other teen, however, may regularly drive your family car.

Driving: Trouble

1. Accidents and/or tickets due to reckless or simply careless driving will result in a temporary grounding from use of the car. For example, a ticket for going ten miles over the speed limit might be a two-week restriction. An exception will *not* be made for driving to work or school,

even though this may cause considerable inconvenience for other family members. When kids can still drive to work or school, "side trips" become inevitable, dilute the effect of the consequence, and cause many arguments.

2. Second episodes of accidents or tickets will involve not only grounding, but also driving lessons that the teen pays for. The driving instructor is asked to teach the child defensive driving, and the teen cannot drive again until at least three lessons have been completed and the instructor says the kid is ready.

3. Drinking and driving, whether or not an accident or ticket is involved, will be followed by a minimum six-month-to-one-year grounding from the car. Community service of some kind may be used to work off not more than 25 percent of the restriction period.

Drugs and Alcohol: Prevention

1. Don't model drug and alcohol use. Evaluate and define your own attitudes toward these activities. If you have an addiction to something like smoking or drinking, admit it to your kids, tell them how you got it, and say that—even though you're trying—it's a hard habit to beat.

2. When the child is younger, have her volunteer at or visit a drug/alcohol rehab center for a while.

3. Ask your kids what they know or have learned at school or elsewhere about alcohol and drug use. Listen carefully and don't get into lecturing.

4. See how many of the following questions you and your teen can answer.

20-QUESTION DRUG TEST

1. How is today's marijuana different from that used twenty years ago?
2. What are the effects and the dangers of inhalants?
3. Why do people try drugs in the first place?
4. What causes people to continue to use drugs?
5. How long do alcohol and marijuana stay in the body?

6. What is the most unpredictable drug on the street today?

7. What is the primary reason that a heroin-dependent person continues to use that drug?

8. Which age group has the highest percentage of drug users?

9. What form of drug use poses the greatest health hazard to the greatest number of people in the United States?

10. What drugs should be avoided during pregnancy?

11. What sobers up someone who is drunk?

12. Is marijuana truly a "gateway" drug or not?

13. What is "crack"?

14. What are some of the effects of LSD and how long do they last?

15. After alcohol and tobacco, what is the class of substances most commonly abused by eighth-graders?

16. What is the relationship between drug abuse and AIDS transmission?

17. What are some of the side effects, physical and behavioral, of anabolic steroid use?

18. What are some of the long-term effects of amphetamine abuse?

19. Name three substances that fall in the depressant drug category.

20. Describe four stages of substance abuse.

5. When you hear of a drug- or alcohol-related tragedy, don't take the opportunity to lecture your kids about the dangers involved. Your drawing obvious conclusions or using scare tactics is not helpful with adolescents. Instead, see what your children have to say about the obvious tragedy and listen to their thoughts.

6. Don't leave your teens home by themselves overnight.

7. If you are going out in the evening and your teens are going to be home by themselves, ask them what they would do if some other kids dropped by who had been drinking and who wanted to continue to party

at your house. Make sure your children have some idea what to say, as well as what to do when calling a neighbor or the police becomes necessary.

8. If your teen is going out, make sure the rules about hours are clear. If you feel there is legitimate cause for worry, wait up for him (alternate parents to spread the burden).

Drugs and Alcohol: Trouble

1. Drug and alcohol problems are best dealt with early, so don't waste time if you feel there is cause for concern. Drug abuse in its advanced stages is extremely difficult to turn around. If you suspect there is a problem, you may want to contact your local health department or a nearby hospital and talk to a drug/alcohol counselor about your worries and what to do.

2. Signs that drug use is a problem include the following:

- unusual mood swings
- change of friends
- suddenly falling grades
- increased irritability
- withdrawal
- sudden secretiveness
- being obviously under the influence
- going through substantial amounts of money with nothing
  to show for it

3. If your teen comes in late at night and obviously under the influence, acknowledge that there is a problem but don't talk about it then. The next morning make an appointment to talk as soon as possible.

4. Your family doctor or a psychiatrist can leave a standing order at an emergency room or the doctor's office for a drug urinalysis. The order should say that the test will be "surveilled," i.e., someone will watch the teen produce the urine. Such tests can be useful as part of psychological treatment, or they may tell you that it's time to get psychological treatment. The best time to have the test done? First thing in the morning after a night of suspicious activities. Calmly tell the teen that refusal to do the test means to you that the results would have been positive.

5. If you are worried about drug or alcohol use, but have good reason to believe that only minor experimentation has been involved, have the child attend an educational program given by an outpatient AODA (alcohol and other drug abuse) clinic, health department or local hospital. Monitor urine for a few months afterwards.

6. What about your kids drinking with you at your house? A sample of wine or a beer for special occasions or toasts is fine. Regular, recreational drinking with you is not.

Sexual Activity: Prevention

The best way to discuss sex is gradually and frequently as the kids grow up, as questions arise and as the topic pops up in daily life. Ideally, sex should be discussed in a way children can understand at their age.

That's a lovely idea and it almost never happens. Kids don't spontaneously ask sex-related questions, and parents rarely take the opportunity to explain something when an issue does "pop up." Our society may be sexually overstimulated, but we certainly aren't comfortable talking openly about anything even remotely related to human reproduction or sexual feelings.

To make matters worse, when parents think about the sex education of their children, they always seem to come up with this funny idea of "talking to the kids about sex." This notion implies some kind of know-it-all parent imparting useful sexual information to an a receptive child who can hardly wait to get the real scoop. Closer to the truth is this: on the one hand we have an anxious parent with imperfect knowledge and a vague idea of where to begin who dreads the idea of talking to his teenage son. On the other hand, we have a teenage son who finds the thought of his parent talking about sex disgusting, and who, quite defensively, thinks he knows all that is necessary anyway.

So what are you going to do? Here are a few thoughts:

1. Don't feel guilty if you get the creeps even thinking about discussing sex with your child.

2. If you're really super uncomfortable, maybe you are not the one to try to discuss sex with your child. Maybe a friend, aunt, uncle or therapist would be better.

3. Whatever they may have actually done sexually, few teens are going to think of themselves as novices as far as sexual knowledge goes. They've been exposed to different information from school, friends, movies and TV, as well as from books and magazines. They may feel—rightly or wrongly—that they're quite well informed.

4. If you say to your teen "Sometime you and I have to discuss sex," and you are met with, "Mom, I already know all about that stuff!" here's one suggestion. Do the Sex Test. The old idea about giving the child a book to read may not be so bad.

Here's how it goes. You explain to your adolescent, "Look. My job may not be to give you all the information about sex. It may be more just to make sure you know it so you don't get hurt. I'm talking about things like getting pregnant (or getting someone else pregnant), forced sex and sexually transmitted diseases like gonorrhea and gruesome things like that. Let's do this. I've got a book with some good information in it. We can both use it for a reference if we need to. I'm going to make up ten sex questions for you, and I want you to make up ten for me. You can try to stump me if you want, but I can try and stump you too. Then we sit down a few times and throw the questions at each other. Of course, we make sure we come up with the right answers. Then you're free to pursue your own existence with no more hassles from me. How about it?"

You may have some studying to do! Find a good book and get going. One such reference is *The Family Book of Sexuality* by Mary Calderone. Find out what you need to know and make up your questions. Or you can use our 20-Question Sex Test:

20-QUESTION SEX TEST

1. At what age is a boy physically capable of fathering a child?
2. Discuss the pros and cons of condoms vs. birth control pills.
3. How is sex related to a guy's ego and to peer pressure?
4. Trick question: do teens get AIDS?
5. Give an objective, three-minute discussion of "acquaintance rape."

6. "You're the first one I've ever had sex with." What do you think of this statement?

7. Samantha may have had sex with 250 people last night. How is the risk of STD influenced by the multiplier effect?

8. Why do condoms sometimes fail to do their job?

9. How would you describe TV's image of sex?

10. How can a young girl handle sexual harrassment at work?

11. How do you figure the time of the month when a woman is likely to get pregnant?

12. What are the symptoms of gonorrhea?

13. How do you say no to a boy in the back seat and not hurt his feelings? What's wrong with that question in the first place?

14. John has just gotten Tammi pregnant. Both kids are 16. What is John's responsibility to Tammi? To the baby?

15. Are STDs preventable? How?

16. Compare the attitudes of a 40-year-old mother or father to a 16-year-old boy or girl regarding sex before marriage.

17. How is AIDS transmitted?

18. What are the differences between male and female sexual arousal?

19. At what age is a girl physically capable of conceiving a child?

20. Why are there one million teen pregnancies—80 percent out of wedlock—each year?

Exhausted? You have your work cut out for you!

Sexual Activity: Trouble

1. If you are worried about STDs and have an open relationship with your son or daughter, you might ask him if he thinks he needs a checkup.

Where a relationship is less candid, other parents simply ask their family doctor to do the appropriate tests for sexually transmitted diseases, without the teen knowing it, the next time the child has a physical. If the results are positive, however, perhaps the doctor, the adolescent and you can discuss it together.

2. If you are worried about sexual abuse, you may ask the sensitve questions, "Has anyone ever made unwanted or forced sexual advances to you?" and "Would you tell me if they had?" Keep in mind that many kids who have been abused still won't admit it. If the child admits that something has happened, it's time for them to see a therapist who has experience with this kind of problem. As a parent, you may be so upset that you need to talk to someone yourself. Always take seriously any child's statements or hints that she has been abused by someone. The absolute worst thing to do is to scold her for making such ridiculous claims. You'll never hear from her again, the problem may never be dealt with, and the abuse may, in fact, continue.

3. Your daughter tells you she's pregnant. What should you do first? First you make sure you do no harm. You and your girl will forever remember your immediate response. You will be shocked and horrified, but you can rest assured that your daughter is in worse shape. Give her a hug. Cry if you feel like it. Ask a few questions.

But no temper tantrums. If you're so upset you can't see straight, wait a few hours before you try to talk. If your spouse goes ballistic, get him or her away for a while.

Next, contact a pregnancy counseling service. Find one that provides actual counseling and not merely abortion screening. Your daughter will need someone to talk to other than you about what to do, and she needs to evaluate her three alternatives: adoption, abortion or keeping the baby. Large numbers of young girls opt for abortion or choose to keep the baby. Far fewer put their babies up for adoption.

4. If your teenage son is going to be a father: in few situations will the relationship between the two adolescents last. Ask your son how he's going to manage the situation, how he can support the girl, and how the decision will be made about the baby. Ask him what you can do to help.

Part IV

Emotional Blackmail

15

Testing and Manipulation

If you are frustrating someone by not giving him what he wants, he has three choices. First, he can decide it's not such a big deal and put up with the frustration. Second, he can make a sincere attempt to negotiate with you. Or third, he can try to test and manipulate you. These are also the options teenagers face when they are being frustrated by their parents. In this chapter we will focus on the third possibility, testing and manipulation, which we have also referred to as emotional blackmail.

Behavior with a Purpose

Testing and manipulation is not unusual or sick; it is a normal but aggravating part of family life. Adults do it and kids do it. People try to manipulate when they are frustrated and when they want to either get something pleasant or weasel their way out of something unpleasant. Your teens will not usually thank you for wanting to negotiate with them, discipline them or in some other way try to direct a part of their lives. Instead they will test and manipulate to see how far they can get. You will get more testing from adolescents as you begin doing things that are more intrusive. When you are only in the observer role, on the other hand, you won't get any testing at all from the kids.

Because it occurs when the adolescent is frustrated, testing is purposeful behavior. Actually, it has two possible purposes. The first purpose of testing and manipulation is for the teenager to get what he wants. Let me go out, don't ask me to do my homework, lend me a few bucks, let me torture my sister, or get off my case about my grades.

The second purpose of testing comes into play if the first purpose fails. If the child doesn't get his way, he will try to get something else. The second purpose of T&M is revenge. The youngster is going to try to make you pay for your insensitivity to his needs.

Being knowledgeable about and prepared for testing and manipulation is critical to successfully parenting your adolescents. It will do little good to put a lot of careful thought into handling a situation if you can't manage the teen's response to what you do. You can't expect your kids to be grateful to you for disciplining or frustrating them.

When anybody "decides" to engage in manipulative attempts to influence another person, he has basically six choices: Badgering, Intimidation, Threat, Martyrdom, Butter Up and Physical Tactics. Except for Butter Up, these stratagems are meant to frustrate the parent in some way. What the frustrated adolescent is implicitly doing, then, is offering you a deal: now that we're both frustrated, you call off your dogs and I'll call off mine.

If you do give the child his way under these circumstances, he will immediately stop whatever testing tactic he was using. Guaranteed. And if you give in like this on a regular basis, you can have him running the house in no time.

Tactic 1: Badgering

When using this tactic, the unhappy camper repeatedly harps at you about what he wants. Over and over and over. The idea is this: to wear you down. "Just give me the stupid car or whatever for tonight and I'll leave you alone" is the basic idea. It might go something like this:

"Dad, can you loan me five bucks?"

"I just gave you your allowance yesterday."

"It's gone, and we're going out for pizza."

"You should have been more careful."

"Come on, Dad, they're picking me up in five minutes!"

"How many times have I told you to think before blowing all
your allowance in one day?"

"The point is they're on their way!"

"What did you do with it?"

"With what? Dad, please—just this once."

"Why don't you ever hit on your mother?"

"That's them! Please—I'll look like an idiot!"

"All right, all right, all right! Just get off my back!"

Score: Kid 5, Dad 0. Dad was caught off-guard, tried unsuccessfully to
argue, then became overwhelmed with sympathy.

Tactic 2: Intimidation (Temper)

The second testing tactic is also aggressive, but it is usually more vicious
than the first. Here the frustrated teen has a temper tantrum, yells, swears,
or accuses you of being a lousy parent. The goal, obviously, is to make you
feel uncomfortable:

"Mom, can I use your lipstick?"

"You've got some of your own."

"I can't find it."

"Then look around. I'm tired of you using and losing my stuff."

"Well thanks one heck of a lot! One simple, stupid, apparently
mental, idiot request and it's too much for precious mother.
Gosh, the level of caring and consideration for others around
this rathole is overwhelming. I'm fainting from too much love!
I'll tell you what you can do with your precious lipstick!"

Quite nasty, wouldn't you say? Intimidation can inspire extreme
anger or extreme fear in a parent. Since this tactic is so unpleasant, parental
anticipation of intimidation sometimes makes Mom or Dad give in to a
demand before the child has a chance to go into her fit. The teen asks for

something, and immediately you have this uneasy feeling in the pit of your stomach: if you don't give her what she wants, all hell will break loose.

Tactic 3: Threat

The third manipulative strategy is Threat. Here the teenage charmer states directly, or implies, that some untoward consequence will befall you—or both of you—should you continue to refuse to grant her extremely reasonable wishes. Should you wish to avoid certain tragedy, on the other hand, the solution is clear and readily available.

Fourteen-year-old Marie wanted to go out to a movie on a school night, but her mother said she had to stay home for her usual study time, especially since she had a biology test the next day:

> "Mom, I can study when I get back."
> "It will be time for bed."
> "I won't be able to concentrate with all of them out there having a great time, and me just here doing nothing."
> "Sorry."
> "You'll be sorry when I flunk this test."
> "You'll do OK if you study."
> "I'm too mad to even think. How am I supposed to concentrate on that stupid biology? It's garbage."
> "Do the best you can."
> "Can't even do one simple thing. You're gonna regret this—you wanna see a lousy progress report—just wait till midterm!"

Marie threatens to not study, then to flunk the test, then to do poorly in the rest of her courses as well. Some kids get even scarier and threaten to run away, get pregnant or kill themselves. The goal of Tactic 3 is to make Mom or Dad anxious. The parent can then eliminate anxiety by giving her daughter what she wants.

Tactic 4: Martyrdom

This tactic may be the all-time favorite of children and adults. Here the unhappy adolescent pouts, cries, looks sad, doesn't talk, doesn't eat, or otherwise indicates that life has become incredibly burdensome since the advent of the new frustration. The obvious cause of the torture, of course, is the teen's irrational parent. Conversations with the youngster may disappear completely, while in other cases they may become quite short. In the next scene, for example, Dad is getting the cold shoulder because he told his daughter she couldn't go to a motel all night after the prom.

"How was your evening?"
"OK."
"What did you guys do?"
"Nothing."
"You get something to eat afterwards?"
"Nope."
"Well, did Mark seem to have a good time?"
"I don't know."

The Silent Treatment. Martyrdom is obviously designed to make the parent feel guilty, and for many adults guilt induction can be a real problem. Martyrdom is more subtle than Badgering or Intimidation, which are usually blatant attempts at manipulation. With Martyrdom the implied message is something like, "Life is hardly worth living since what you've done to me, and you don't deserve to be talked to anymore. But don't worry about me, I'll handle my life from now on by myself."

Unfortunately, some parents have a "guilt button" the size of the state of Wyoming, and it is all too easy for their children to press it and get whatever they want. If this type of guilt-prone parent tries to escape the emotional discomfort by giving in, however, he often simply trades his guilt for anger when he realizes—once again—that he's been had. In our example above, if Dad doesn't shut up soon, he's going to dig a big hole for himself.

Tactic 4 is sometimes hard to tell from genuine clinical depression. There are differences, though. Depression will be more persistent and will exist even when the child is not being frustrated. A depressed teen may not enjoy anything. Martyrdom will occur from time to time when the child *is* frustrated. A teen who uses Martyrdom periodically can still enjoy herself the rest of the time.

Tactic 5: Butter Up

This testing tactic is different, because it is the only one of the six where the adolescent doesn't make you feel uncomfortable. Here they make you feel good! Sort of.

With the Butter Up routine the child may compliment you, promise you something nice, or complete some rather unusual chore around the house. But there is a catch: you are expected to reciprocate by either not frustrating him in some way or by giving him something he wants . If you don't respond correctly, you may observe with fascination (and horror) the quick transformation of Butter Up to Intimidation or some other negative testing strategy:

> "Well I cleaned up the garage. Can I have the car tonight?"
> "I didn't ask you to clean the garage. In fact I just did it last week."
> "Well, there was some junk lying around. What about the car?"
> "Your mother and I need it."
> "For what?"
> "It doesn't make a lot of difference, Brandon, we have to go out."
> "Well thanks a lot. You know, you try to do something nice around here for someone and what happens? You just get dumped on!"
> "Watch it, buddy."
> "You watch it! I'm sick and tired of having to stay around here all the time while you guys cover the globe anytime you want. Why the heck don't you fix that other piece of garbage in the driveway so I can go out once every year or two?!"

Here the token garage cleaning was obviously manipulative and, unlike the other testing tactics, it preceded the potentially frustrating event. Butter Up, however, is often hard to tell from genuine affection or consideration, so you have to evaluate it carefully. In fact, there is certainly nothing wrong with making a deal—beforehand—that if the garage is cleaned up, the teen can use the car. Such an agreement would be true negotiation rather than Butter Up.

Tactic 6: Physical

One of the worst forms of testing and manipulation—and, fortunately, probably the least common—is employing physical measures to get your way. These actions can include attacking other people, breaking things and running away. Adolescents who use physical tactics can make life pretty scary for you.

Kids who use physical strategies to get what they want often have a history of this kind of behavior. Physical tactics are not uncommon, for example, in conduct-disordered kids. This kind of conduct may also come from ADD or depressed children. Parents who encounter physical testing often become vulnerable to another testing tactic: Threat. The threat of physical harm or damage can certainly make you think twice about sticking to your guns with a frustrated teenager.

In young children, testing and manipulation tactics may inspire parental reactions that range from feeling irritated to feeling amused. With teens, however, testing may produce responses in Mom and Dad that involve substantial aggravation as well as fear. How are parents to manage these youthful maneuvers without either feeling like tyrants or like they are capitulating?

16

Managing Testing
and Manipulation

M anaging testing and manipulation is not easy, but you'll do a lot better if you first recognize testing for what it is. Labelling the kids' manipulative tactics in your own mind while they are happening is very helpful. "There's another example of Martyrdom," or "I might have known—the usual list of threats"; or "Here we go again with the Badgering." Next you must understand the basic principles regarding how T&M works. And finally, you need to know exactly what to do and what not to do when confronted with the manipulative efforts of your youngsters.

Important Basic Principles

Several basic considerations become apparent when you reflect on the purpose of testing and the different tactics kids can use. If an adolescent frequently repeats one particular form of testing, you probably are not handling it well. Why? Because people naturally tend to repeat behavior that works for them. Check first to see if you are reinforcing manipulative behavior by caving in and giving the teen what she wants. Second—even if you are sticking to your guns—check to see if you're getting so upset that your teen is enjoying exquisite, satisfying revenge. Either response will make her want to use the same tactic again.

As you get better at not giving in, the kids, in their increasing frustration, may either escalate one tactic or switch tactics, or both. The temper tantrums may get worse for a while if you suddenly decide you are no longer going to give in to them. Or the adolescent may switch tactics on you—even during the same conversation—trying, more and more desperately, to find one that gets through:

"Can I use the car tonight?"

"No, I need it."

"What for?"

"Have to go shopping."

"Can't you do it tomorrow?" (Badgering)

"No."

"I'll put some gas in it." (Butter Up)

"Can't do it."

"Come on, for Pete's sake, just for two hours. Why do you have
  to be such a pig about it!" (Intimidation)

"How many times do I have to tell you you can't have it?"

"See if I'm home when you get back." (Threat)

"You can go fly a kite for all I care."

"Fine, I'll just sit in this excuse for a house all weekend."
  (Threat/Martyrdom)

This kind of pressure is aggravating and somewhat scary, but keep in mind that tactic switching is a sign that you are doing better at not giving in.

A fundamental, logical principle of testing management is next: don't give in *after* the teen has started testing. Giving in then is a wonderful way to reinforce aggravating behavior. This rule does not imply that you shouldn't grant some of your kids' reasonable requests *before* there is any reason for testing. If you have doubts or reservations about an adolescent's request, tell your daughter to give you a few minutes to think it over, then you will give her your response. Tell her to be ready either way, and also let her know that *testing during your deliberation will axe the deal.* If your answer is "No," be prepared for the worst and keep quiet.

Finally, if you continue to remain reasonable and firm in handling requests and testing tactics, escalation and switching will decrease over time. Eventually the kids will grow more accustomed to your being firm, they will know what their limits are, and—believe it or not—they will be happier. Why? Because by definition T&M means they are getting upset too. The more they use these strategies, the more upset they will be. As you become more reasonable, consistent and firm, both of you will be happier because the frequency, intensity and duration of hassles will be less.

Exactly how do you handle adolescent manipulation? We'll get to that in the last section of this chapter. Before that discussion, however, we must be honest and admit that teenagers aren't the only ones in the house capable of testing and manipulation.

Testing and Manipulation by Parents

Kids aren't the only ones who try roundabout strategies in order to get their way. When parents are frustrated or can't seem to get through to their kids any other way, Mom and Dad sometimes slip into using some of these tactics themselves.

Tactic 1: Badgering. The parent version of this is one of the Four Cardinal Sins, Nagging. When parents nag, it doesn't always have the same urgency as when kids do, but it's still a form of Badgering. Nagging expresses frustration and the almost psychotic delusion that repetition will solve the problem.

Tactic 2: Intimidation. A parental favorite. Yelling and screaming, though, don't really solve many problems. They are often a sign of emotional dumping—common when a State of War exists.

Tactic 3: Threat. Using this tactic can mess up the Major/Minor System in a big way. You don't want to threaten something that you're not going to do. You'll begin to lose your credibility, unless empty threats have already blown it for you. Don't say, "You're not going out tonight if your room isn't clean" if you don't mean it.

Tactic 4: Martyrdom. Another parental favorite, especially when parents feel powerless or intimidated by their teens. When you are feeling like nothing else will work, why not try some heavy-duty guilt induction? This tactic may be a little less prevalent since the phrase "guilt trip" became popular, but many parents still use martyrdom a lot. Since most children are notoriously unappreciative of their parents' efforts, Martyrdom, unfortunately, has a certain kind of emotional logic to it.

Tactic 5: Butter Up. Parents—like kids—don't use this one too much. It's too easy for the adolescents to see through it.

Tactic 6: Physical. Mom and Dad don't use this one much either with teens. If they do, however, we may have a problem with child abuse. Mom or Dad may also get hurt themselves during physical encounters, which usually leave everyone feeling terrible afterwards.

The 'Guilt vs. Anger' Problem

An interesting dilemma, which is both very common and very upsetting, arises in the course of many close relationships, such as husband/wife or parent/child. This dilemma occurs when one person inadvertently offers another person the choice of whether he wants to feel angry or guilty. This predicament involves a kind of competition between two people and between two testing tactics: Intimidation (#2) and Martyrdom (#4).

Here's how it goes: 13-year-old Kristina walks into the family room where her father, Mr. Applegate, is busy watching his favorite football team. With an innocent question, Kris offers her father the choice of whether he wants to feel angry or guilty:

> "Dad, can you drive me to Jenny's?"
> "Kris, that's clear across town."
> "It will only take 40 minutes."
> "You know, you pick the worst times to ask me for rides."
> "Your stupid football's more important, huh?"
> "Why the heck can't you ever plan ahead?"
> "You never do anything with me anyway!"
> "OK, OK. Let's move before the stupid game's over."
> "No, no. Hate to ruin your day. Thanks anyway—I'll just stay home!"

When his daughter asks him for a ride (a spontaneous request, by the way), Mr. Applegate can either take her and feel resentful, or he can refuse and feel guilty. The choice is clear; what to do isn't.

This type of emotional choice occurs frequently in all kinds of relationships. It's fascinating to note that when people have to choose between feeling angry or feeling guilty, they usually prefer anger. Perhaps the reason is that when you are angry, you are thinking someone else messed up, but when you're guilty, you're thinking you messed up.

Whatever the reason, the two people involved often wind up sort of jockeying for position, trying to take the angry position and at the same time put the other person in the guilty role. When Dad, for example, says, "You pick the worst times..." or "OK, OK. Let's move before the game is over," he is really saying, "I'll be angry and you be guilty." But Kris isn't about to stand for that, so she comes back with, "Your stupid football is more important" and "I'll just stay home." She, in other words, is now saying, "No way, buster! I'll be angry and you be guilty." If Kris does stay home, she may become the official winner of this match: she can be angry and Dad will feel guilty.

You're probably thinking, "This sounds pretty stupid." It is, but it happens a lot. Isn't there a more rational solution than two people trying to "guilt" and manipulate each other to death? Certainly it would be better to negotiate (or to plan ahead). Perhaps Dad could have responded by saying, "I can take you if you can hold on till halftime."

If you are the parent on the receiving end of a spontaneous request like the one above, or in some other situation with your teen that might involve this kind of jockeying, your best bet is to say "no" or make a reasonable counteroffer. Then—if the teen is still unhappy—live with the guilt if you have to and avoid coming back with intimidation to eradicate your discomfort (check out Mom's reaction to Deedee in the example coming up).

Managing Testing and Manipulation

Back to testing and manipulation by teenagers. Exactly how do you handle it? The answers can be found in our earlier discussions of the Four Cardinal Sins and the Major/Minor System.

For the more verbal tactics, such as Badgering, Intimidation, Threat, and Martyrdom, don't get baited into spontaneous discussions, arguing, or lectures (you usually won't have to worry about your nagging because the teenager will be doing the nagging). There may come a time in the conversation when you have to just shut up, even if your offspring is still going at it. You may even have to leave the room. You may have to just stand there—saying nothing—while you keep doing the dishes. It doesn't feel very good, but there's no point in talking anymore.

Mom does a good job in this example:

"Deedee, your clothes aren't down here for the wash."
"Can you get them for me?"
"No, I can't."
"Mom, I'm right in the middle of this show!"
  (Silence)
"Give me a break, will ya!"
"Sorry."
"Oh for pete's sake, I gotta do everything around here." (Goes
  to get clothes)
  (Silence)

It's very hard not to get tricked here into some lecture about responsibility or about who really does all the work around here, but in this interchange Mom is the model of self-restraint. It's silence or "This conversation is ridiculous, I'm outta here!"

For more drastic verbal and for Physical testing tactics, the Major/Minor System should be invoked. Things such as swearing, big-time name calling, staying out late or smashing household goods require consequences. Look back at our Major, Medium and Minor categories and decide which would be appropriate. Words by themselves seldom merit a Major consequence, but breaking things might and physically hurting someone else would. If a child is acting this way on a regular basis, some kind of professional evaluation might also be in order.

For both repeated minor as well as major episodes of testing, sometimes it is helpful to use negotiating. Here the problem being discussed is testing itself. In counseling sessions we have had some very interesting conversations about this subject. First we show the kids and the parents the list of six testing tactics from *Surviving Your Adolescents*. Then we ask the teens: "Which ones are your favorites and which are your parents' favorites?" Next we ask the parents the same question in reverse. If you try this with your children, be ready to admit that you are not perfect either and may use a little T&M from time to time. Don't try to have this discussion on the spur of the moment, of course.

Living with teens on a regular, day-to-day basis, you must always be prepared to handle one or more of the these six tactics. If you are not, you are engaging in wishful thinking and simply setting yourself up for trouble. When confronted with testing, have you ever said, "Why can't you ever take 'No' for an answer?" "I'm sick and tired of your hassling me all the time" or "You're never happy unless you get your way, are you?"?

It's almost as if parents who say these things are expecting their kids to appreciate Mom or Dad's efforts to raise them and to be thankful for any discipline provided. Get a life!

And be prepared.

Part V

House Rules

17

Guidelines for
Specific Problems

Below are some suggestions, using the ideas in *Surviving Your Adolescents*, for handling the problems originally listed in the Introduction. What is suggested will sometimes vary depending on the age of the teen and your overall feeling about his or her competence. If you already have a good solution, forget the advice in SYA and stick with yours. These ideas are only suggestions, not rules.

Arguing

This is the number one problem parents of adolescents complain about. What these complaining parents often forget is that they control 50 percent of an argument, since it always takes two people to produce one. Many times arguments continue because each person has to have the last word. Mathematically speaking, if you have two people arguing, and each insists on having the last word, you have a potentially infinite discussion. Ad nauseam, as they say.

Arguing shouldn't happen if you are studiously avoiding the Four Cardinal Sins. Arguing is useless and provocative. Sometimes active listening can help abort an argument, then negotiating might prove useful if there is a problem that needs to be resolved. If you're getting yourself too angry, cool off and think before trying to talk again. If you are regularly having too much trouble keeping quiet, you are probably doing a lot of emotional dumping

Arguments will rarely help get your point across. Say what you have to, if necessary, then the subject. Remember that in the entire history of parenting, no teenager has ever responded to a parental tirade with a sincere, "Gee, I never looked at it like that before."

Bedtime

For the younger 13-to-15-year-old adolescent group, if there is a problem, the best method is simple advice, especially for competent kids. If the problem persists, negotiating may be the next logical step. If the child persists in going to bed ridiculously late, or bothering other family members, the Major/Minor may have to be used. Some really weird sleeping schedules can be related to drug use or depression, so these suspicions sometimes need to be evaluated if the problem continues in spite of every attempt to modify it.

For older teens, even problem kids, stay out of their sleeping habits unless the child is disturbing others at night or the teen's sleeping schedule is just so unorthodox that he is obviously suffering from it. Problem children will probably have other more important difficulties that you need to worry about.

Bumming around town

This area is controversial, but we suggest giving the kids some leeway. During the day or early evening, letting your average 13-to-15-year-olds hang around malls or downtown areas is fine. Ask them to tell you where they are going and make sure hours are clear. Some parents require a call if the kids change places, but this request is difficult for most teens to comply with. It's probably best not to insist on a call, unless the kids want to go someplace far or risky.

Older kids can tell you where they think they are going and that's it. No calls are necessary unless they are going out of state or someplace similarly monumental. Parties would be covered by the rules agreed upon for that (see Parties: home and away on page 156), and hours must be respected. Don't grill the kid: "Where are you going, with whom, what are you going to do, whose idea was that, what if this happens, how much money do you have, where's your coat it's cold out there and I think you're catching a cold," etc. Your adolescent, you recall, will be less safe if she leaves the house angry with you.

What about kids who have already been having problems with bumming around? They don't go out for a while, according to the rules of the Major/Minor System. Then you give them some rope, and if they goof up, it's another grounding for a short, defined period. Then let them try again. It's hard shutting up and not grilling the teens before they go out. You are anxious and you want some reassurance, but you will just irritate your children with all your questions. It's worse to have an Irritated Problem Kid going out. If you want, the kids can tell you where they are going and whom they'll be with, and that's it.

Car: care, use, gas

There are many arrangements possible. For more competent teenagers, free use (if there are enough cars) is reasonable, and the child pays either all or half the gas. Competent kids might even be allowed to buy their own car, provided they pay the insurance and their grades stay good. Many insurance companies have 25 percent discounts for kids who maintain a B average in school. Some families have the adolescent pay the extra if she doesn't keep the B average. Don't make this arrangement, though, unless you're sure that your son or daughter is capable of that level of schoolwork in the first place.

Linking car use to grades is fine, as long as the deal is defined precisely. For example, the teen can use the car whenever he wishes, provided he maintains a C+ average (2.75 on a four-point system) with no Fs for any quarter or progress report. If he drops below that, the use of the car is restricted temporarily (define the time) until he gets his GPA back to 2.75. If you have a difficult child with marginal school performance, no car on week nights (except for rare special occasions) is a good idea. No drinking and driving, and hours must be respected.

Care of the car (changing oil, checking tires, etc.) is something of a problem, because many kids don't know much about mechanical problems. Dad usually winds up taking care of general auto maintenance, which is fine. If the child is interested and wants to learn, negotiating the deal would certainly be a good idea.

Chores

Negotiating is probably the best place to start with chores. Attempts at advice too often turn into nagging. Sit everyone in the family down, divide the chores up, and if you want, hook up some of the allowance to the chore (you have to keep track of who did what). Avoid making spontaneous requests about chore-like tasks. Parents are always saying things like, "I only asked you to do one little thing, what's the big deal?" The big deal is that everyone—including parents—hates to be interrupted.

"But he never does anything he's supposed to!" Some kids are just naturally forgetful. Nagging won't help, but if you don't do something, you'll feel angry and martyrlike. A good option is the "Docking" system, which was discussed before as a version of the Major/Minor System. You have a problem with Mike feeding the dog regularly in the evening, although he had agreed to do it (Mike is 14 and gets an allowance of $8). Simply tell him the dog should be fed by 6 p.m. If the dog isn't fed, you will do it. But, you charge 50 cents to do a feeding. If you don't get to it right at 6:05 and Mike beats you to it, there's no charge. No reminders! You can use the same procedure for laundry, dishes, messes around the house, and straightening bedrooms.

Many parents find it easier to just do things around the house themselves. That way things get done and they get done right, right? There's probably nothing horribly wrong with this approach, but you have to be careful you don't become a Major Martyr and then expect everyone else to respond with enthusiasm to your requests for "help" on the spur of the moment.

Church

If you haven't done much about attending church before, you're probably not going to start when your kids are age 13 or more. Modeling is important here: you can't expect them to go much if you don't. For 13-to-

15-year-olds, your involvement here is optional and it depends a lot upon what your religious beliefs are. It probably isn't a good idea to go past negotiating for a child who is giving you a real hard time by not attending church. Grin and Bear It, and keep quiet about it on Sunday mornings.

For older teens, staying out of the issue is your best bet, perhaps after one shot at consulting. For some people, having their child talk to their pastor or minister alone has been more helpful than the teen talking to his parents. Many times if the kids talk to someone outside the family, they are on their best behavior and also are much more reasonable.

Appearance

This is true MBA territory. Keep in mind that for many adolescents their appearance is designed to look weird and to shock you. If you have a fit about it, you're playing right into their hands.

With any teens, the best advice is probably to tell the kids that they can wear anything the school will let them in the door with. This statement isn't necessarily saying a lot, because schools these days will put up with some pretty horrendous outfits. The furthest you should go in most situations is just giving advice. Otherwise Grin and Bear It. Even if your son comes home with a huge, colored, dangling earring.

You would not want to allow your child to wear a T-shirt to a wake, however. Some kids have tried it! But you also can't dress them. If necessary, give some advice or try talking it over in situations like this. If all else fails, don't sit with him, don't let anyone else know he's yours, let him stay home, or treat it as a Minor or Medium infraction.

But remember: "Styles change, Mom!" If the adolescent's wearing something really weird, try to deawfulize it and keep in mind that she very likely won't be dressing like that ten years from now. In addition, with difficult kids, you certainly don't need any extra hassles.

If the school is actually not letting the child in the door because of dress, that's a different story. It must be quite an outfit! You certainly should consider going to the Major/Minor System.

If you've already had a set of rules for hairstyles and dress, and your adolescents are used to them (no regular arguments or other hassles), forget the advice here and keep doing what you're already doing.

College plans

For older adolescents, advisor and negotiator roles are appropriate. After all, you most likely have to pay for room and board and tuition, or at least for a lot of it. Tell your daughter what your financial limits are and look at some possible schools together. It's amazing how many parents seem to just let their son or daughter pick a school, then Mom and Dad try to figure out a way to pay for it. When their relationship with you is fairly good, many kids need and appreciate advice, direction and support.

Depression

Genuine depression is always a serious problem. It can also run in families, so family history is important to pay attention to. Other signs of depression include:

1. Pervasive gloom
2. Difficulty enjoying anything
3. Irritability
4. Low self-esteem
5. School underachievement
6. Social withdrawal
7. Appetite disturbance
8. Sleeping disturbance
9. Being slowed-down or tired all the time

If you feel you have a depressed teenager, it's time to consult a professional. Do not try to diagnose or deal with this problem yourself.

Family outings

A lot of times your teens no longer want to join you on family outings. This change is perfectly normal. For the younger teenagers, working out some kind of a deal may be a good idea, because you may not want to leave them home alone. Punishment for not going may at times be appropriate, but you'll usually have a sullen kid on your hands if you force him to go. Consider doing nothing, leave him home and enjoy yourself!

Older teens can decide for themselves if they want to go with you.

There shouldn't be much problem leaving them home by themselves. If they goof up when you're gone (like having a huge, wild party at your house), of course you'd use the Major/Minor program.

Friends and dating

We suggest staying out of your kids' choice of friends, except under dangerous circumstances. If you don't like some of your children's friends, you might try a little advice or even some negotiating. Part of the problem here is that it is next to impossible to control—especially with older teens who drive—whom your child sees out of the house. In addition, when poor parent/child chemistry exists, your trying to stop a relationship with one of your teen's undesirable friends may only serve to make their bond stronger.

If you can stand it, invite the creep over to your house and see if you can get along with him. Some of these kids aren't so bad once you spend some time with them! For example, many parents find out that what had passed as arrogance was really shyness in disguise. If the other child is, in fact, a bad influence, you certainly can use the Major/Minor System on your child for whatever trouble he gets into. In desperate situations, where you are sure the other child is having a very bad effect, you might actually use the Major/Minor for your son's merely getting together with the other teenager. Many parents don't let their kids date until they're 16 years old. Others let the child date, but not alone in a car until they're 16. Parents can chauffeur, or the kids can go out in groups. Violations are handled with the Major/Minor. If your teen is going out on a date, always meet the other party beforehand.

Grades and homework

With competent children and temporary drops in grades, merely watching and doing some listening might be all that is necessary. Negotiating a positive reward system (like money for grades) has been used with success to help wake the kids up, but the Major/Minor System by itself is not always so useful since it involves only punishment. "You're grounded until you get those grades up!" is a strategy that, if it's going to be used, needs to be very specific (e.g., the grounding ends when you achieve a

GPA of 2.5 with no F's). Any motivational system like this, however, should also have some positive reinforcement attached to it. Though rewarding a difficult teenager is never easy for frustrated and angry parents, it works a lot better.

Negotiating set study hours—with no phone interruptions allowed— is often helpful for kids who are struggling. Believe it or not, many adolescents can study better with their radios on (it blocks out other distracting noises), but never with the TV.

Try not to be checking the child's work all the time. If you insist on this perverse procedure, be sure to use a lot of positive reinforcement and don't insist on perfection. Tell her what she did right on her assignments! Hooking up the use of the car, as well as more freedom during the week, with a periodic, specifically defined grade check can also work, provided you don't argue about the arrangement. Write the deal down on paper.

If all this fails, a professional evaluation, and perhaps psychological testing, may be necessary. Coming up with a diagnosis of learning disability, Attention Deficit Disorder or something else may shed light on the situation, but remember that, by the time they're teenagers, a lot of water has already passed under the bridge.

Grammar

It's a little late.

Hours

Hours should be clear for all ages, though for kids in the 16-to-18 group who are generally doing well, considerable flexibility is OK, as long as it's not abused. For younger teens, staying in on weeknights during the school year is a good idea for average or difficult kids, unless there is some special reason for them to go out. With competent kids, going out is not a problem, and you might use the bumming around suggestions above.

What hours are reasonable? We usually suggest sticking with local curfews. This often means something like 11 p.m. on Sunday through Thursday and midnight on Friday or Saturday, and this kind of setup also takes a little of the burden off parents.

What about violations? For first-time offenses, just give the kid some friendly advice. With continued problems, however, a handy and simple system is the following:

1. 15 minute grace period.
2. If he is over 15 minutes late, the child must "pay back" the minutes next time he goes out—he must come in that much earlier. If he was 25 minutes late, for example, he must come in 25 minutes early the next time.
3. Over 45 minutes late, he must pay back double time.
4. Over three hours late, one week grounding or consider it a Medium or Major offense.

Don't grill the adolescent when he comes in late: "Where were you?" "Why can't you ever get home on time?" etc. You may just be asking for a lot of lies or other forms of verbal refuse, which makes it harder for everyone to get to sleep afterwards. Inform him of the consequences the next morning.

Music

Trying to control the quality or nature of the music the children listen to is probably a lost cause. Trying to deal with its volume may not be. Of course, if you are strange enough yourself that you too enjoy adolescent musical preferences, then there is no problem.

Advice can get tedious and quickly turn into nagging: "Turn that blankity-blank thing down!" If you don't like this noise pollution, negotiate a deal such as sharing the cost of earphones. When someone else is home, for example, the youngster must wear the earphones. If that doesn't work, small fines may be more useful. If fines fail, temporary removal of the stereo (e.g., one-day removal after three unsuccessful warnings in one day) should follow.

Meals and eating habits

Rigid adherence to attendance at nightly family dinners is less and less appropriate as the child gets older. Suggesting that he be present at four of seven evening meals each week might be a reasonable idea, but his not showing up should not trigger the Major/Minor System. It might be better to go back to merely being an observer. Nagging about coming to the dinner table is not allowed, no matter what you cooked.

What the child eats should be handled the same way. Suggesting that he eat three of the four foods available often works well, but if the teen wants something else, the answer is either "No" or "OK, but you'll have to get it, pay for it and make it yourself." Will the adolescent clean up the kitchen after he cooks something for himself? Of course not. Use the docking system if you get stuck with his mess.

Sloppy eating habits have never been nagged away. Try some friendly advice. If that fails and the kid's really obnoxious, don't eat together. Attendance at meals and manners are not earthshaking issues; and with problem children, trying to do something about these concerns is often more trouble than it's worth.

Messy rooms

Close the door and don't look. This is perhaps the all-time, classic MBA. Her room is her territory and there is no research demonstrating a relationship between sloppy rooms in childhood and lack of success, homelessness or criminal activity in adulthood. Two problems arise here: dirty dishes and laundry. If she doesn't get her laundry down to the washing machine once a week on Saturday morning, it doesn't get washed, or she can do it herself. Teens should learn to do their own laundry anyway, since their parents already have enough to do. If you have to pick up dirty dishes from her bedroom, just charge her ten or 15 cents per item and forget about it.

Money, allowance, loans

Allowances are helpful for two reasons. First, they can be used as incentives for chores and other tasks. Second, they can be handy when fines or the Docking System are being used (such as for swearing), and you would like total control over the consequences.

How much is reasonable? Who knows? But here are some *very rough* guidelines: for 13-to-15-year-olds, about four to eight dollars per week; for 16-to-18-year-olds, eight to 12 dollars per week. Consider continuing the allowance even if the teen gets a job (you may need some clout), and by all means, encourage her to get a job as soon as she is old enough. It's great for her independence and for her self-esteem. One caution: some research indicates that teens who are in school should not work more than 20 hours per week during the school year.

It's preferable not to get involved in how your adolescent spends his money. Let him learn through trial and error the benefits of saving vs. the pitfalls of impulsive spending. In situations where the kids are planning to go to college, many parents require that the child save one half of all earnings for his college expenses.

If you are not telling the child how to spend his money, you also should not regularly provide "loans" to bail him out when he's short. There's no problem with helping your teen out on occasion. But when these so-called loans become gifts, you will be subsidizing irresponsibility.

If you do make loans, keep them small and set up a strict payback schedule. Make sure it's clear to begin with whether the money is a loan or a gift, and don't make additional loans until the first one is paid back. If the kid is defaulting, garnish his allowance. As you negotiate these financial arrangements, keep an eye out for the cancer of righteous indignation in your attitude.

Negative attitude

Some kids, it seems, were born crabby. They just appear always to be in a bad mood or to have a chip on their shoulders most of the time. Many other people—adults included—are generally in good spirits, except in the morning.

One of the worst things you can do is try to cheer up one of these non-morning people. Your "Isn't this going to be a nice day!" at 6:50 a.m. will be met with the unprintable. Let your child stagger around unmolested.

If the negative attitude is something new and persistent, consider some gentle active listening to see what's going on, or even professional counseling if the attitude appears serious, quite different and enduring. Remember that continued irritability is frequently a sign of depression in kids. Never chase a martyr, however. If the teen is nonverbally "broadcasting" that he is upset about something, and your "What's wrong?" questions are always met with "Nothing," you are stuck. Instead, say "It looks like something's on your mind. If you want to talk about it, let me know." Then turn around and walk away.

Parties: home and away

For younger adolescents, parties are no problem if you're there. For older, competent kids with whom you get along well, you might allow a party if you're not home only for extremely limited numbers. Use negotiating first to clarify ground rules, and don't go too far away! Explain what to do if the party gets out of hand (for instance, call the police), then ask your kids if they would really take these actions if they became necessary.

No drinking is allowed. If you find out later that someone was drinking, that person either spends the night or gets a ride home. If your own party is crashed by too many people and you can't handle it, call the police. If you've had repeated problems with parties in the past, just say "No" when your teens request another one, explain once and prepare for testing.

Kids any age can be allowed to go to a party where the parents are home. Call beforehand to make sure the parents will be there. Expect a good deal of flak from your child about this, and comments like, "All my friends think you guys are weird. Everybody else is going." If the parents aren't going to be home, your kids don't go to the party. Imagine you have a problem child who wants to go to a party where the parents won't be home. You tell him no. He accuses you of not trusting him. You tell him nicely that he is correct.

Phone

As all parents of adolescents know, phones are obnoxious devices that we all could live better without. In order to help magnify the curse, however, modern technology has also provided us with the benefits of call waiting, caller ID, answering machines, voice mail and cellular phones. Added to these aggravations are 900-numbers that some adolescents have used to ring up hundreds—or even thousands—of dollars "worth" of sex calls, which their parents don't find out about until the phone bill arrives.

You pretty much have to put up with incoming calls, but a negotiated or imposed rule about incoming calls after 10 p.m. or so is reasonable. The kids can tell their friends to cool it after a certain time.

If most of the calls coming in are for your kids, don't answer the phone yourself. It's a waste of time. Let your youngsters break their own necks dashing for it.

If the phone bill is too high, some families have the kids share the cost. If the kids get their own phone, they should pay for it themselves, especially the older group. If it's a separate number, the p.m. hours restriction may be relaxed; if it's the same number, the same rules apply.

Fights among the kids about phone use are reasons for a family meeting. Write down the agreement.

Too much time on the phone should be dealt with first by doing nothing. Leave the kids alone. Teens are supposed to spend a lot of time on the phone! It's good for them!! If their dialogues, however, are seriously interfering with other family members' use of the phone, or the child is doing poorly in school, then advice, negotiation or even Minor consequences might be appropriate.

For the sex calls, local phone companies have a service that lets you restrict the area codes that can be used from your phone. When *you* need to call a number within a blocked area code, though, you can use a four-digit number before dialing to get through.

Sibling rivalry

There is no cure for sibling rivalry. It is amazingly aggravating and persistent. Next to arguing, sibling rivalry is the problem parents of adolescents complain about most frequently.

Involvement here may be optional, if you can stand the noise. Remember that sometimes these squabbles are a harmless pastime for the kids, even though they can be a major aggravation for you. Also try to keep in mind the rule that says your level of anger about a problem is not always the measure of its seriousness. Sibling rivalry may be an MBA, and you can let the kids work it out themselves.

If you can't stand it—which is certainly understandable—or if one of the kids is really getting hurt, emotionally or physically, by the fighting, you should intervene. Most parents probably do. The counting procedure from *1-2-3 Magic* may still work well. After one or two unproductive warnings, you separate the combatants for 15 to 20 minutes in their rooms. Remember: never ask what happened or who started it (absolutely the world's dumbest question) unless someone is physically hurt, and don't expect older children to be more mature than younger when it comes to household battles.

Smoking

Ideally, of course, no one should smoke. Don't model it, first of all. If you insist on smoking, don't do it at home or just do it outside.

Next, if there is a problem with smoking, start with negotiating. Listen first! Active intervention should be used with 13-to-15-year-olds. Use the Major/Minor if they are smoking, but remember you have very little control over what they do outside of the house. Don't grill them—if you smell smoke on their breath, just impose the consequence with no yelling or lecturing.

For older adolescents, drop the Major/Minor System but insist they smoke only outside the house so the rest of the family are not "passive smokers." Smoking in the house is a Minor or Medium offense. One of the best strategies here may be to avoid the Four Cardinal Sins and to try to improve your relationship with the adolescent. Hostility toward parents helps fuel a lot of teenage smoking.

Swearing

If you're modeling the words you're telling your kids not to use, you've got a big problem. You can't very well tell teenagers not to use certain words when you do in front of them. Some families set up a "swear jar" and simply fine anyone, parents included, for bad language. Anyone who swears has to put 25 or 50 cents in the jar; at the end of the week the money is donated to church or charity. This method seems to work well for many families; in fact, the kids enjoy turning the tables on their parents occasionally and this setup also motivates them not to swear themselves. If you don't swear yourself, a simple fine system that varies with the "badness" of the word may be the best idea.

You may legitimately feel that you're fighting a losing battle with the problem of swearing, because the kids' friends, music and movies usually use these words frequently. Though you can't control what the teens do outside of your home, you can have some say about how they talk when they're with you.

Behavioral trouble at school

Behavioral problems at school, such as disrupting or cutting class, and smoking in the washrooms, require your involvement. The Major/Minor System can be used if it doesn't involve too much double jeopardy (punishing the teen after the school already has). With average or competent kids, these kinds of problems are not likely to be chronic or severe, so for first-time offenses you may just use a little advice.

With difficult kids, however, school behavior is often a large part of their overall problems, and a professional evaluation and counseling may be warranted. What if counseling has already been tried and it didn't do any good? You could try to find a different therapist, or you might be stuck with crossing your fingers and avoiding the Four Cardinal Sins.

Using your things

Kids borrow clothes, misplace tools and use up your makeup, deodorant and shampoo. They also like your glasses, wristbands, jogging shoes, diet pop and pens. This type of "borrowing" usually is not a big deal, so in many cases some friendly consultation may be adequate. Why not consider it a compliment—the little creatures are identifying with you!

Nagging and screaming do no good at all. How "Awful" is it, really? Rate it from 0 to 100 on the Awful Scale before you do anything. If you have a chronic problem, try to negotiate some kind of deal or simply outlaw the use of your stuff. Violations may be handled with simple fines. If all else fails, borrow some of their stuff.

Vacations: kids stay home

You want to take a vacation and leave the kids home. You just saw the movie *Risky Business*. What should you do?

"We don't need a sitter—what do you think we're babies?!" "John's parents let him stay home by himself when they went away." That's what your adolescents will tell you.

Don't listen. With younger teens, you get a sitter—an adult or college student—though you might consider leaving a competent 17- or 18-year-old in charge. Be sure you negotiate things like locking up, use of cars and—most importantly—friends over. Either no friends come over while you're gone, or set a limit of one or two extremely reliable teens.

What about sibling rivalry while you're gone? That's the kids' problem, provided no one gets hurt. Stay in touch.

Work

Getting and holding down a job is an excellent experience for teenagers. It's a great introduction to the real world and can do wonders for a person's self-esteem. Teens with jobs have their own money and learn something about responsibility, supervision and getting along with others. A job can also help them get out of bed in the morning during the summer.

If your son or daughter has problems at work, you should stay out of the situation if you can, though active listening and lots of positive reinforcement may be helpful. If the teen is looking for a job, don't nag her about it. You may circle job ads in the newspaper if she doesn't find this assistance irritating.

Occasionally a supervisor may call you about a problem your adolescent is having. It's a good idea to try to stay out of the middle. If you can, tell your adolescent who called and what the person called about, and then ask your teenager how she thinks she will handle things.

First we'll try negotiating...
I'll go first, we have a better relationship...
if that goes bad we'll have to go
to MAJOR/MINOR!

18

SYA in Action

L et's examine a few hypothetical examples to get a better idea of exactly how parents might apply some of the ideas we have discussed. Each example will be preceeded by a kind of "snapshot" of the situation, stating what the problem is, what sort of adolescent we are dealing with, how well the teen gets along with his or her parents, and how the parents would rate their own well-being on a 1-to-10 scale (10 is great, 1 is lousy). Following each example, we'll evaluate how well the problem was handled.

SNAPSHOT:
Problem: smoking
Child: competent 17-year-old
Relationships: good with mother, poor with father
Parents' self-ratings: mother 7, father 5

Damon is smoking between one-half and a whole pack of cigarettes per day. His parents are aware of this habit, because he sometimes smokes at home in his room or when other people aren't home. His father used to smoke until three years ago; his mother never did. Damon claims his smoking doesn't worry him and that he finds it relaxing.

Damon's parents have talked to him about his smoking, and there have been a few arguments. Mom has pointed out the obvious health hazards. Dad has described to his son how he himself stopped. Damon has listened, and he has even acknowledged the value of some of their points, but he has not altered his habit.

After reading *Surviving Your Adolescents*, Mom and Dad decide they will have one attempt at negotiating. They feel there are two problems: Damon's smoking is a hazard to himself and the passive smoking is a hazard to other family members. The parents decide that for the first problem they will attempt to negotiate, and if that doesn't work, they will then keep quiet and Grin and Bear It.

For the second problem, however, the Mom and Dad decide that Damon shouldn't be allowed to impose his smoke on the rest of the household. So if talking doesn't work, they will use the Major/Minor System if necessary.

Because Mom has the better relationship, she asks Damon if they can go out for ice cream or yogurt some night to discuss the problem. Damon loves yogurt. He agrees. Mom and her son discuss the problem at TCBY. Damon does not want to stop smoking, but he agrees not to smoke any more in the house, provided that both mother and father get off his back about the problem. Mom agrees to communicate this idea to her husband.

Comment: Mom and Dad did very well. The good relationship Mom had with her son made their talk a lot easier. The parents' conference with each other before doing anything was also an excellent idea, especially since Dad and Damon don't get along too well and run the risk of merely arguing.

Follow-up here will be very important. Will Damon be able to quit smoking in the house, or will there be need for another negotiation or consequences if he can't? Will Mom and Dad be able to keep quiet?

SNAPSHOT:
Problems: bedtime and homework
Child: average 15-year-old
Relationship: average with mother
Mother's self-rating: 5

Dynna is a sophomore in high school. Her grades are generally C's, though her mother and her counselor feel she is smarter than that. She usually stays up at night reading novels unrelated to school and doesn't go to sleep until about 12:30 or 1 a.m. In the morning she is often somewhat irritable, and has said she sometimes almost falls asleep in class. Mrs. Phillips rightly feels that her daughter's lack of sleep is hurting her emotionally as well as academically, but she doesn't quite know what to do about the problem.

It is 12:15 a.m. on a Wednesday in October. On the next day Dynna has a history test which she hasn't studied for very much. Returning from a late snack in the kitchen, she wakes up her mother, who meets her in the hall outside her bedroom door.

"What are you doing?"

"I just went down to get something to eat."

"You should have been in bed a long time ago—don't you have a test tomorrow?"

"I was in bed."

"That's not the point. Those stupid romance novels aren't going to get you an A in history."

"At least they're more interesting than garbage!"

"Listen to me! Fifteen long years on this earth doesn't give you the right to screw up your life. From now on, I want your lights out at 11 o'clock at the latest—you hear me!?"

"Of course, mother dear." (Slams door)

Comment: This discussion was a waste of time and worse. Mom was, understandably, caught off-guard on this particular night, which is partly why she makes three mistakes: 1) a spontaneous "problem-solving" discussion, 2) no active listening before an attempt at a solution, and 3) a premature jump to the director role. Compliance here is not very likely, but further battles are in the offing.

In addition, mom's general stress level and the parent/child relationship do not allow for a confrontation like this to be productive, especially when two problems—bedtime and homework—are being discussed at the same time.

What should Mom do? A little work on the relationship might help, then a brief attempt at consulting. If that doesn't work—and it probably won't—it's time to move on to negotiating, because the problem is important. Any future conversations between Mom and daughter, of course, should be planned in advance, especially since their relationship is only average. This incident is a good example of the poor results that occur when problems are discussed on the spur of the moment.

SNAPSHOT:
Problems: arguing and use of car
Child: average-to-competent 16-year-old
Relationships: good with mother, rotten with father
Parents' self-ratings: mother 8, father 2

Beaver and his father are continually going at it, primarily about one thing: the gas in the car. Beaver doesn't seem to realize that the needle can rise above one-eighth. Dad does, because he's the one who is usually "filling the blankety-blank thing up to the top" in addition to filling up his car and his wife's from time to time. This situation irritates him, and with good reason.

Dad naturally wants to explain a few things to Beaver about life, but the kid doesn't ever listen:

"You use the car?"
"Yeah."
"How come there's no gas in it?"
"There's gas in it."
"Oh really. Wanna know how empty that tank is? If I threw a match in it, nothing would happen!"
"I'd like to see you try it."
"OK, wise guy, now you listen to me..."

Comment: Another case of righteous indignation. How about a little active listening, Dad? No way. Beaver is certainly messing up, but—with their rotten relationship and Dad's general stress level—Dad is so far from being able to do active listening it isn't funny. He and Beaver will just use each other for target practice, unless Mom steps in.

Mom and Dad should sit down together—without Beaver—and decide what to do. Mom then implements the plan and reports back to Dad.

Things may be too far gone for any advice giving, so Mom might try negotiating a deal first. If that doesn't work, it's on to the Major/Minor. Also, Dad needs to decide if he should address any problem with his son at all. If he does bring something up, it would be helpful if he asked himself if he's really trying to solve a problem or really trying to start a fight. It sounds so far like his true goal has been the latter, and his warlike attitude will probably affect areas other than car use.

SNAPSHOT:
Problem: sibling rivalry
Child: average 15-year-old
Relationships: average with mother, excellent with father
Parents' self-ratings: mother 5, father 5

Jorge describes his little seven-year-old sister, Paula, as a total brat. The two of them can't seem to be in the same room without arguing. The fighting sometimes gets physical. Paula will then cry or scream, and Mrs. Michael will run into the room to try to put out the fire. Though Jorge gets along better with his father, Dad travels a lot and is not around to handle most of the squabbles. No amount of talking or arguing or lecturing has ever done any good. The kids just keep at it, and seem to almost consider their battles a pastime.

Finally, Mrs. Michael consults with her husband. They read *Surviving Your Adolescents*, then decide to do the following:

1. In most fights, they will discipline both kids; if the fight is bad enough, both children will be asked to go to their rooms for ten or 15 minutes.
2. They will no longer ask what happened or who started it.
3. They will not expect Jorge, because he's older, to act more mature during an argument, though there will be increased consequences if he physically hurts his sister.
4. They will not expect the fighting to stop, realizing both kids enjoy it to some extent, but they will hope to cut down the frequency of the battles.

Mom talks to Paula, and Mom and Dad take Jorge out to dinner by himself. They discuss many things, including the new rules. Dad explains that even though he can't be home all the time, he expects Jorge to follow the rules and his mother's instructions. If he doesn't, it will be back to negotiating, then Major/Minor if necessary.

Comment: Good thinking. Mr. and Mrs. Michael are using a version of the director role, since discussing sibling rivalry with the kids was a waste of time. They are also being realistic in not expecting an older child to be more mature when it comes to fighting, and also in not expecting sibling rivalry to stop—ever.

SNAPSHOT:
Problem: drinking and pot
Child: average-to-competent 16-year-old
Relationship: average to good with mother
Mother's self-rating: 5

Triton has always been a pretty good kid, as far as Mrs. Tiegen is concerned. He even seemed to survive the recent divorce fairly well. Lately, however, he has been "hanging" with a new crowd and staying out later. He also has been showing some signs associated with drug or alcohol use: uncharacteristic irritability, coming home and going straight to his room, a drop in grades, and what sometimes sounds like slurred speech on the phone if he happens to talk with his mother after he's been out for a while.

Mrs. Tiegen has tried some advice, mentioning that she doesn't care for his friends too much, suggesting that sometime he invite them over for her to meet and asking him directly if he is drinking or using other drugs. She has done a pretty good job of avoiding the Four Cardinal Sins, but she is getting more and more worried. In their conversations, Triton is usually pleasant but evasive, and if she pushes the talk he becomes more irritable.

Mom decides to try talking things over, knowing she's unhappy with Triton's friends, grades and hours. She tells him she would like to talk sometime and suggests they go out for dinner. She is determined to start out by briefly stating her concerns, then she will use active listening to try to get more information.

Triton and his mother go to a drive-in—his choice—and are sitting in the car after eating:

"You said there was something you wanted to ask me?"

"Yes, ah, I'm worried about how your doing. I think you've handled the divorce OK, but lately you seem to be different. Frankly, I'm wondering about your friends and about your drinking or using other drugs."

"Mom, give me a break!"

"That doesn't help me very much."

"Well, what do you want to know?"

"I just told you what I'm worried about."

"Sure, I've had a few beers with the guys and smoked some joints, but I don't see what the big deal is."

"You don't think it's any problem?"

"Hell, no—everybody tries it sometime or other."

"Well, I have to admit, I'm a little surprised—though maybe I shouldn't be. (A bit teary) Give me some time to think, and maybe we can talk again, OK?"

"Whatever."

Comment: Mom is off to a good start with a difficult problem for her. She has her thinking cap on, has done a good job of listening, cut off the conversation when she got upset, and laid the groundwork for future talks. She has not at all condoned what her son is doing, and may need to set down some rules later, but her first job is to get reliable information about what's going on and to establish a basis for talking.

SNAPSHOT:
Problem: bumming around
Child: 14-year-old problem child
Relationship: poor-to-rotten with both parents
Parents' self-ratings: mother 3, father 2

Ramona has been having all kinds of difficulties for the past year or so. Her parents aren't doing so well either. Sometimes it feels as though—in this family—no one gets along with anyone. It's Saturday and Ramona wants to go bumming around at the mall, but Mrs. Rider may have other ideas:

"I'm heading off to the mall with some friends."

"Are you asking or just telling me? Don't just come waltzing

in here and inform me about what you think you're going to
do, young lady."

"All right. May I please wend my way, using extreme care,
to the shopping mall, with a few of my better-behaved
acquaintances, dearest mother?"

"Watch it, sweetie. I don't like the idea: go talk to your
father."

"Talk to him yourself! I'm sick of this crap!"

Comment: Nothing is going right here. This is a clear instance in
which the parent and the adolescent have two totally different ideas about
what role Mrs. Rider should have regarding her daughter's desire to bum
around. Ramona thinks that Mom should be in the observer-only mode,
and Mom seems to feel that she should be taking charge and have the final
say about whether or not her daughter goes out at all. Mom is correct but
didn't handle the situation well.

Ramona certainly has been having her problems lately; if these have
included difficulties while bumming around, then she shouldn't be going
anywhere for a while. On the other hand, if her going out with friends has
been no problem, she should be allowed to go in spite of her other
difficulties. Ramona says where she's going, with whom, and respects her
hours. Mom doesn't grill her further. If problems come up, the deal
changes.

It's now several months later. Mom decided she wasn't doing so well
herself, so she went to see a therapist. Her husband was not interested in
going. After several months of counseling, and also with the help of some
antidepressant medication, Ramona's mother was feeling much better and
thought it was time to deal with her daughter. At the suggestion of her
therapist, she tried to sit down with her husband and discuss Ramona's
problems, but he got extremely angry—as usual—and lapsed into his
"She'd better shape up or else!" routine.

Finding no help there, Mrs. Rider read *Surviving Your Adolescents*
and came to the conclusion that her relationship with her daughter was too
bad for them to be able to do any kind of constructive talking. Instead, she
figured she'd better spend some time working on how the two of them get
along. Since her husband was a lost cause, the pressure was on her to try

to do something. She decided on the safest route: asking Ramona to go with her to dinner and a movie. She knew her daughter would just about faint with surprise at the request, but Mom was ready and did her best to get into an active-listening frame of mind:

"Sometime, ah, you feel like just you and me going out to a show, and then, ah, getting maybe something to eat after?"

"Are you talking to me?"

"Believe it or not."

"You going nuts or something?"

"Nope. Serious."

"You gotta be kidding. (Laughs uneasily) You and me could never agree on a movie in four godzillion years!"

"You pick."

"Folks, the lady has lost her mind! The butter has definitely slipped off this woman's noodles."

"What show sounds good?"

"I got it—the old let's talk at Ramona routine. The litany of past sins over a hot fudge. Dairy Queen psychotherapy. I'm not interested. Nope. No thanks."

"I promise no talking about problems. I will not even once mention your hair or your grades, but you have to do the same, OK?"

Comment: Three cheers for Mrs. Rider. She has truly shocked her daughter, and she also showed, at least for the time being, that she is doggedly determined to avoid war. Is Ramona weakening? She sounds somewhat intrigued by her mother's weird new behavior, but she is obviously very mistrustful.

This one's going to take a while.

SNAPSHOT:
Problems: money and loans
Child: competent 18-year-old
Relationship: good with father
Parent's self-rating: father: 6

"Dad, can I borrow $150?"

(Cough) "Sorry, musta been something I ate. What?"

"No, come on. They're having a sale on these CD players, and I'm short a little."

"Wait a minute. Didn't we give you your allowance a few days ago? And what happened to your last paycheck—you can't be out already?"

"I'm not out, I'm just low."

"Do you owe us any money now?"

"No, I'm all caught up."

"If I loan you the money, how do you want to pay it back?"

"With snakeskins. No, just kidding. With my paychecks. I could give you $20 a week for seven or eight weeks."

"OK. Even though you may not feel it's necessary, write out the deal on paper—it's a loan, not a gift, and I'll see what I can do about getting some cash."

Comment: Good example of negotiating. Dad doesn't get cranked out of shape by a spontaneous request, and also makes it clear what the deal will be with the money. The teen sounds like he's good for it.

SNAPSHOT:
Problem: depression or just a bad mood?
Child: average 15-year-old
Relationship: good with mother
Parent's self-rating: mother 5

"Life sucks!"

"That's what I like about you, your constant good spirits."

"No, I'm serious."

"Well, why do you have to bother me about it?"

"'Cause you're so easy to torture. No, I mean like everything's a real bummer."

"Did something just happen to you?"

"Something isn't the word for it. You wanna know the incredible stunt that Wendy just pulled?"

"What?"

"Well, like, I'm at work—busy to the max—and she calls,

and she's like 'Oh, poor me, what am I going to do. Do you think you could do just one small favor for me?'...etc., etc."

Comment: Good recovery by Mom. It's amazing her daughter stuck around for it. It's time for some active listening. It looks like just a bad day, rather than a major case of depression.

And now one last thought before you get to work...

Part VI

The Future

19

Ten Years from Now

W hen your adolescents are acting up, it's easy to get worried about how these "kids" are going to turn out when they are adults. Will they ever make it to adulthood in the first place? If so, will they be able to survive on their own? Here are a few final thoughts.

Straight Thinking

Remember that adolescents are in the business of being different from you. They may even want to shock you from time to time. They have a lot of energy and they want to try a lot of different things.

Though they worry their parents from time to time, teens are not yet the people they are capable of becoming. They are still in the process of development: experimenting, learning and changing. For most of these kids, these changes will be positive. In ten years you will not have the child you have today—you will very likely see an independent and responsible adult.

Supporting this hope are some interesting facts. One was the study, mentioned earlier, that found periodic acting up during your teenage years isn't all that bad, as long as you don't "O.D." on it. As that research indicated, the "experimenter" type of adolescent was both normal as well as emotionally healthy.

Another interesting piece of information suggests that most adolescents are constructively learning about life during their transition years. Conduct-disordered teenagers, as mentioned before, are a difficult crowd. Yet by the time they hit adulthood, more than 50 percent of them have reformed! They no longer act out like they used to. They learned a lesson—often on their own and without professional help.

If even CD kids can learn from their experimenting, fooling around and getting in trouble during their adolescent years, it certainly seems reasonable to expect that our average and competent teenagers are going to do an even better job of sorting out their lives. Did you ever learn something valuable from "activities" that your parents never knew anything about?

Get Ready for the Future!

Another interesting thought is that in ten years your 13-to-18-year-olds will be 23-to-28-year-olds! The majority of these young men and women will be married, raising families, going to school, working and living on their own. Eventually, just about all of them will be as much a part of our social fabric and work force as you are now. These 23-to-28-year-old women probably won't have partial crewcuts and blue hair, and their opposite sex peers, on their way to work, probably won't be wearing pants that are falling off.

Finally, 10 years—or less—from now something else could happen. You could become a grandparent! If the kids live close, you could actually have the opportunity to babysit your grandchildren frequently!! Imagine chasing several two- or three-year-olds around your house while the toddlers' parents are relaxing at a motel over the weekend. Now let's see, where was it that we left that copy of *1-2-3 Magic*?

Index